From my Heart and Soul

Betty Jean Holt

Betty Jean Holt
11-15-10

Copyright © 2010 by Betty Jean Holt

From my Heart and Soul
by Betty Jean Holt

Printed in the United States of America

ISBN 9781609579623

All rights reserved solely by the author. The author guarantees all contents are original and do not infringe upon the legal rights of any other person or work. No part of this book may be reproduced in any form without the permission of the author. The views expressed in this book are not necessarily those of the publisher.

Unless otherwise indicated, Bible quotations are taken from the King James Reference Bible. Copyright © 2000 by Zondervan.

www.xulonpress.com

Preface

I was encouraged to write my memoirs several years ago, mainly by my daughter-in-law, Sherle. I wondered, what I could say that would be interesting enough, to keep anyone's attention. I felt that I had lived a rather dull life. After all, who am I? After Jerry's parents and my Dad had passed away, there were times I wished I could have asked them a few questions about their life. So with that thought, I began writing.

A few weeks ago, on a Sunday night, I listened to my oldest grandson, Ryan, minister at church. As he spoke, he asked three questions. What has God done for you? What is He doing for you now? And what will God do for you in the future? In other words....What is Your Story? He told us that some of the things we've gone through in our past is "our story." At that point, I was glad to be telling *my* story. I'm at this place today because this is where God wants me. When my children and grandchildren go through tough times and perhaps might wonder where God is, I hope they can look back at these pages and see how God brought me and their Grandpa through similar times. I realize we pass through this land only once. Whatever we do we need to do well. Lost time cannot ever be regained. Make your life count.

I want to pay a special tribute to the man I love. Jerry your strength and faith has been a strong arm for me to lean on.

Even with your disability, you think of me and tell me daily how much you love me.

You have given me encouragement to finish this book and tell the story, "From My Heart and Soul."

Chapter One

The Early Years

Although I have never lived it down, I can remember sucking a baby bottle. We lived in a house on Highway 1, just north of Wynne, Arkansas, where I was born. The house was green and had a bedroom with the bed beside two windows. Mama would fill my bottle with milk and then put Karo syrup in it. She would lay me on the bed and I could watch the cars go by on the gravel highway outside. I loved the taste of the milk and to this day, sweetened condensed milk reminds me of it. When we moved from that house, I was nearly three years old. Daddy told me that a little boy was moving in after us and I should leave my bottle for him. I remember where I left it sitting as we drove away.

We were moving to a brand new house just a few miles away. It was owned by a man named Mr. Hawk. Being the youngest, I really got all the attention. My sister Bobbie and two brothers, Dewey and Giles, went to school and I had Mama all to myself every day. My first recollection of Christmas was at that house. I lay awake thinking I heard Santa outside. I was scared and could not sleep....a feeling most kids experience at least once in their lifetime. The next morning, I found a baby doll under the Christmas tree! We lived just down the road from my Grandma Childers. On that particular Christmas, I received a pretty blue ribbon (about 12 inches long) from Grandma. It was not wrapped, just put in a regular envelope and sealed. Didn't matter, I thought it was beautiful **and** my favorite color. In thinking back on that gift, I realize how she must have sacrificed to give something to all her grandchildren. Times were hard and she was a widow with not much income.

We had neighbors named the Caudells. I played with their children and I guess I had learned a new word and didn't realize it. One day we were playing dolls at their house and I commented that my baby was constipated. When the adults laughed at me, I thought I was cute. I have no idea how I learned the word. I must have heard it from the adults in my house. Of course, back then, discussing things like that was not done in public, especially by children. I would have been in trouble if Mama had heard me say that.

Mama let me help her pick blackberries. The summer was hot and I got covered with chiggers. She would lay me near the front door on a pallet and pick the chiggers off. The breeze was always cool there and I would fall asleep.

When I was five years old, we moved about 4-5 miles away. The house sat up on a small hill. There is nothing left of it today. I had the chicken pox while we lived there. Mama must have waited until they had about dried up, then she told me, if I would get up very early and scare the chickens off their roost, the pox would leave me. I had her wake me up before daylight the next day. I did as she had told me, and sure enough, within two days I was cured! I was too young to realize that I was almost over them when she told me to do that.

Christmas was quite eventful that year. Christmas Eve was on Sunday night. We always went to church and that night we all got in the car except Daddy. I figured he was in the outhouse. Finally he came to the car and we went to church. After the service we came home to find that Santa had been there!! I got a tricycle that year and Giles got a bicycle. Dewey got a basketball and Bobbie got a wristwatch. Our stockings were filled with nuts, fruit and candy. Those things were not plentiful during the year but we always had them at Christmas. Daddy must have harvested a good crop to provide the goodies we had. I was never able to figure out how Santa came while we were gone. I questioned Mama about it even after I was grown. It didn't seem like Dad was in the house long enough to place everything and fill the stockings.

A memory of my Dad during Christmastime was the fact that he always liked to eat an apple and chocolate cream drop candy at the same time. I can still see him pare an apple and pick up the pieces with his pocket knife as he ate the chocolate. I tried to imitate him and got hooked on the combination. I still love it to this day. However, back then, I wasn't allowed to use a knife!

From my Heart and Soul

Chapter Two

My Life Changed

When I was six, we moved just down the road into a little four room brick house. I didn't mind the move because it was in walking distance. My best friend was named Belinda Davis and we could still play together. Her folks owned a little country grocery store. Mrs. Davis would always treat us to a Coke (in the small bottle) and a Hostess Twinkie. I never had money but always got the same treat as Belinda. One day while I was playing there, Daddy came to get me and said that Mama had me a baby brother at the Clinic in Wynne. I had been the baby for seven years and kind of liked the position. They named him Don Anthony. I remember when they brought him home. I wanted them to take him back. I had never asked for a baby brother. He cried and cried. Mama said he had the colic. I stared at him in amazement wondering just *where* he came from. Why didn't they get a girl baby or one that didn't cry all the time? He finally outgrew the colic and stopped his crying. I think he was about 35 or so!! A little humor!

Not only was my youngest brother born, but my oldest brother got married while we lived there. I liked his wife and got to go and visit them at times. Her name was Ruby. She kept some neat things on her bedroom dresser. I can still remember what her brush and comb looked like. She kept a very neat house. Their home seemed a lot more fun than ours. I guess they gave me attention and also, I got away from that crying baby! Life in that little brick house left me with many memories. Years later, my husband Jerry, and I, along with Don and his wife Marilyn, went there to look at the house. It was falling in and a little dangerous. Due to the sagging roof we did not walk in very far, but the memories of the time I lived there came flooding back. I dug deep into the ground near the porch and got a large rock and took it as a reminder. I still have it.

One day I was told we were going to move again. It broke my heart. We moved less than 10 miles away. The only good part was that I still rode the same school bus and went to the same school with all my friends. We had to walk quite a distance to catch the bus. Bobbie and Giles would go on ahead and leave me to walk it by myself. I saw several snakes and lizards as I walked the road to the bus stop. One day as we got off the bus, our neighbor and his little girl offered me a ride home. I was feeling bad and didn't know what was wrong with me.

By bedtime it was evident. I had the measles. They were the bad ones. I was very sick and missed several days of school.

Living at that house was fun. I was free to roam the area and loved it; however, I missed my friend Belinda. There was a pond a few hundred yards away from the house. The pond always looked muddy. I couldn't swim and Mama and Daddy warned me to stay away from it. There was also an area of gullies (okay youngsters, look it up in the dictionary) near the house. I loved to play in them. Sometimes after a hard rain there would be water in the gullies and Mama would let me sail a paper boat. It was not deep and I wasn't afraid. My imagination took me away....to where, I can't remember, because I didn't have much knowledge of the outside world at that age.

Dad let me plant some corn that spring. I dug up an area about 3 ft. by 3 ft. It was so exciting to see the corn shoot up from the earth. I was so proud of my corn. For a seven year old girl, this was quite a crop!

Years later, Jerry and I went back to see that house and it was in bad shape. As we looked through the windows, the rooms looked much smaller than I had remembered. I wanted to go inside, but by then several red wasps had taken up residence there and I sure didn't want to disturb them.

I told Jerry about the pond and he said he didn't see any evidence of a pond being there. I began to walk in the direction I had remembered and sure enough there was a small amount of water still there. My, how the memories came flooding in!

Chapter Three

A Major Move

One day, Dad and Mom decided that we would make a major move to northern Illinois. It was hard to make a living being a share cropper and Dad had heard where he could get a job on construction that paid good wages. He and Bobbie made the trip to Illinois. Dad got the job on construction, rented a house and came back to get the rest of us and our things. He left Bobbie at E.P. and Lydia Holt's house so there would be room for Mom, Dad, Giles and myself to ride in the truck when we made the move. Oh yeah, they brought Don too. He was almost a year old and by then, he didn't cry much!

In July of, 1951, we said goodbye to Dewey and Ruby and started off in a pick-up truck and trailer, headed for a town called Rochelle. I moved away leaving my little plot of corn, really uncertain of my life from then on. The trip took us 24 hours to get there. The roads were two lanes and we stopped in a parking area so Dad could sleep some. Dad, Mom, Giles, Don and I were crowded in the cab of that truck. I know we must have driven Mom and Dad crazy. I had never ridden more than a few hours at a time before that. My Grandpa Banton lived in Jonesboro, AR (about 60 miles from us) and we would get up before daylight to go visit him. To me that was a *looong* trip. Well, here we were on our way to Illinois. To me, it may as well have been to the other side of the world.

When we arrived, Mom was very upset because there was an outside toilet and she was counting on indoor plumbing. The house was in the country on a paved major highway. The old man who owned the place didn't like children and said we could rent the house for just a short while. Our life was so different. We didn't stay there long. It was 8 miles south of Rochelle and Dad wanted to be closer to his work and Mom wanted to live in a town. She had never learned to drive and we only had the truck, so she was home bound all week.

I didn't see a problem because we had lived in the country all my life. I think Mom figured the move to Illinois would be her Utopia.

Sometime before school started in September, we moved to a little town called Creston, which was about five miles east of Rochelle. Dad had rented us a three bedroom, downstairs apartment. Oh dear, another place without indoor plumbing. Mom was so upset again. I couldn't understand why, because we had never had it before!

We were promised the upstairs apartment in a couple of months and it had an actual bathroom. Stool, tub and sink... hurrah!! We did get that apartment and enjoyed the tub. I had never had a bath in a real bath tub in all my life. We always took baths in a galvanized wash tub. We all used the same water, until it was to dirty, then Mom would heat more and the next one got their turn. It was a Saturday ritual and mostly Saturdays only. My grandchildren would shudder at the thought!! I can remember seeing my Dad wash his face, arms and neck at the outside pump, in between his bath on Saturdays. After a year we moved back over to Rochelle and stayed there for just a year. Then, Dad was able to buy us a cute house of our own about 10 miles away in Ashton, Illinois.

From my Heart and Soul

Chapter Four

My Heart Throb

Just before leaving Rochelle, I met the love of my life. His family had left Arkansas and had moved to Rochelle a year before our move. Jerry Thomas Holt was the cutest boy I had ever seen. He had curly black hair and the darkest brown eyes. His smile was a mixture of shyness and mischief combined. He stole my heart. At that time in my life, we had a young man and his wife as our Pastor. She played the piano and they sang together. I was only 10 years old, (going on twenty I thought) but I secretly prayed every night that Jerry and I would someday get married and he would be a preacher and I could learn to play the piano. When I was 12, after much begging, Dad bought me an old upright piano and I started practicing every day. God taught me and I just picked it up and kept improving. By the time I was 13, I was playing in church for the singing. Also, by the time I was 13 I had gone with Jerry Holt and another couple for a Sunday afternoon ride and I was in heaven. On Sundays after church, I would go to a friend's house. Her name was Betty, also. We would go for an afternoon walk and guess who we'd run into? We always got a ride home. Mom and Dad never dreamed Jerry and I liked each other so much. Our families had known each other since before we were born. He was allowed to pick me up for church and take me home to our house in Ashton. We would go to a ball game or school event together. He had always been my brother, Giles' best friend. Now, he was *my* best friend!

We had an older couple come to our church to serve as Pastor. They took time with us and showed us they cared. Brother and Sister Sam Edmunds became our good friends. Jerry was always a little shy around people and never said much in public. When he was 16 years old, God called him to preach the gospel. It was thrilling to hear him tell about the night when God woke him up from a sound sleep and spoke to him about preaching the Word. Jerry argued with God telling Him that there was no way he could stand in front of people and speak, let alone preach. The Lord impressed him to go into the living room and open the family Bible. It fell open to the scripture in 1st Corinthians 2:1-5. Jerry accepted the call, but it was hard to live a Christian life, for we had no real teaching. Years ago, everything was a sin, or so the church thought. They told us what we couldn't do, but not how to live a victorious life through Christ.

Even with Brother Edmunds' encouragement, Jerry began to run from God and from his calling. We tried to live a Christian life, but hopped up cars was our thing, the faster it went, the better. Drag racing was a thrill to us and Jerry's car could always win. I have ridden with him at speeds of 120 miles per hour. When I think back on these times, I know God had His hand on us or we would have been killed. Jerry's life revolved around me and his car. I think it got his mind off the Lord and he didn't have to deal with his calling. We really weren't bad kids, just reckless I guess.

Chapter Five

Life Takes a Major Turn

In those days kids very seldom got any teaching about sex. The schools certainly were not allowed to teach us. We learned from other kids and most of what we heard was incorrect. Jerry and I thought we loved each other and it didn't seem so bad when I lost my virginity to him. Oh, we knew it was wrong but things always seemed to go too far. It wasn't long until I realized I was pregnant. Fear struck my heart. I knew my Mom would probably kill me *and* Jerry. I broke the news to him and he said he'd talk to my Dad and ask if we could get married. Jerry was honest, Dad was not happy, but he was a gentleman and talked to Jerry as a man and not an eighteen year old boy. Mom was not quite so forgiving and was not happy with us for a long time. We married on Valentine's Day in 1959. The wedding was simple but pretty. Most people said it wouldn't last 6 months, but we have celebrated our 50th anniversary…..so I guess it's going to last!

    Our early married life was spent running from God. Isn't it strange how we think we can hide from Him? He had His hand on us all the time and we didn't realize it. The first few months were rough on us. Jerry had a good job working in Rockford, Illinois for Strandquest Motors. He was the assistant manager of the parts department. This was a job he loved. His Dad was a truck driver, but, wanted to open a gas station. He wanted Jerry to work there and oversee it. It was a bad decision, but Jerry gave in. He and his Dad had never agreed on anything, and Henry, as the boss, caused Jerry a lot of grief. Henry could be mean at times and was a hard man to get along with. But, I guess he had a good heart. Henry always seemed to like me and he and Louise accepted me into the family even under our circumstances. He also liked to play practical jokes and was always out to get a joke on me. There were a few times I paid him back, but then he didn't see any humor in that!!

On August 21, 1959, our world changed when Jeffery Thomas made his entrance. I thought this bundle was the cutest baby ever born. (A Mother's love is blind, for he was not that beautiful.) He blossomed into a handsome brown eyed, blond haired boy. I regret some decisions I made in my life, like the lack of will power, lack of judgment and hurting my parents, but I was proud to be a Mother, even though I was very young. I tried to be a good Mother and found Jeff to be the light of my life.

An elderly minister lived across the street from us. He had been our pastor many years before, when we lived in Arkansas. One day he knocked on my door. I asked him inside and he said, "I came to see that baby boy." I took him to the little crib and in his humorous way he said "well, the little thing looks almost human." Of course, he was joking with me, but I didn't think it was funny. It took a long time before I could get over that joke.

We had purchased a very small, furnished, mobile home shortly after we married. Our families had given us some nice gifts at our wedding reception and we didn't need a lot of other things. Jerry was still working for his Dad at the gas station and usually had to close at night. I was left with a lot of spare time on my hands. On a late afternoon in September, I was feeding Jeff and all of a sudden Jerry came driving up in the company jeep and almost parked on the porch. I asked him what he was doing home so early. He replied, "I just felt like coming by to check on you guys." We talked baby talk to the baby for a while and got him to smile. I looked outside and things looked strange. I commented to Jerry how quiet and still it was. In just a few seconds things changed drastically! The wind began to blow hard and it sounded like a train coming at our home. Along with the high wind, the rain came pouring down. Jerry yelled, "Bet, get down" as he pushed me down off the couch and I hovered over the baby. Suddenly, the front door of the trailer was sucked opened and the neighbor's propane tank blew into the doorway and was spewing gas. Jerry grabbed me up and guided me to the bedroom and told me to crouch down by the bed while he tried to get the tank removed. It would not budge! Just after we got to the bedroom a large piece of wood came crashing through the window where I had been sitting just minutes before. Jerry came and hovered down over us and said that live wires were sparking all over outside and with that gas spewing, we could be blown up. The noise was terrible and our home was being moved around. I was scared to death! We said "I love you" to each other and I prayed for God's mercy. I faintly heard a voice calling "Betty, Betty, are you in there?" It was Jerry's Uncle Ray Holt who lived across the street. He was afraid I was at home alone. With Jerry's help, he managed to get the tank out of the doorway. By that time it had stopped spewing gas. The roof of a small cottage had blown off and was leaning up against our trailer and we had to tunnel our way out. I grabbed the bedspread to wrap Jeff in and we ran in the pouring rain across to Uncle Ray's house. Aunt Bessie helped me to get dried off. With a full tummy, the baby had gone to sleep and slept through the whole thing. Soon the storm was over as quickly as it started. The wind had stopped and the rain was coming down lightly. We had survived a terrible tornado with winds at around 100 miles per hour. Jerry and Uncle Ray went out to survey the damages. It was bad! The jeep that Jerry had parked "almost on the porch" had been completely lifted up and a large piece of someone's roof was under it. It looked like a shingled throw rug. When I look back at the bravery of Uncle Ray to run over, in the very strong wind and pouring rain, I am amazed. Of course, Uncle Ray and Aunt Bessie were like parents to us, so that feat actually was not surprising. We realized that God must have urged Jerry to come home when did. I don't know what I would have done if Jeff and I had been there alone.

Finally, Jerry quit working for his Dad and found another job. Still running from God's will, our world almost stopped on Labor Day in 1960. Our folks wanted Jerry to attend the Bible School at Lee College, which was our church affiliated college. We had gone to Cleveland TN, to look over the campus. After being there for a short while, Jerry said, "lets get out of here; I'm not going to school down here." We drove on to Rome, GA, to visit Jerry's Uncle and Aunt, Walter and Eva Wright. The next day they took us to Look Out Mountain in Chattanooga, TN. We spent the whole day there and went back to Rome.

Jerry thought we should start back home around midnight. We traveled a lot at night. That way, Jeff, being a year old, would sleep through most of the trip. When we got near Monteagle, TN, the Lord came knocking. The car left the road and we turned over and over and over. During one of the turns, Jerry cried out "I surrender God." The car stopped on its top with the side resting against a huge boulder. It was barely daybreak and we couldn't see much around us. We couldn't get the car doors to open. We were terrified, because we didn't know where Jeff was or if he was alive. Our head lights were shining a beam up through the sky and a trucker from Alabama saw it. He came sliding down the mountainside to help us. He managed to get us out, and Jeff was safe, but angry that we woke him up so roughly! When the trucker got me up to the road and in the headlights of his truck, he said to Jerry, "man, her head is split wide open." It actually wasn't but with the facial injuries

I had, it looked that way. My face was cut up and I had teeth missing and a huge lump on my head.

Jerry had some broken ribs and a broken nose (probably the Lord punched him!) Jeff had one little bump on his forehead.

Even in the surrender, Satan still had a hold on him. All through Jerry's life, he had suffered physical and mental abuse from his Dad. Through most of his life, he had been severely beaten with anything Henry could get his hands on. He was constantly told that he was no good and worthless. Henry had always humiliated him in front of men at the gas station and treated him like he was a child. I saw Jerry changing. Hatred had built up in his life and I was frightened at times. Satan was out to kill him. Jerry even tried to take his own life on 2 or 3 occasions. One night after church had been dismissed; he went to the altar to pray. No one wanted to stay and take the time to pray with him, except my Dad, who realized what had happened. An evil spirit had entered into Jerry and was the cause of his despair. Dad prayed for Jerry and soon some of the people gathered around to pray also. Never before, had I seen anything like what I am about to describe.

I watched and cried as Jerry's neck became large and his eyes became totally bloodshot. He screamed out "leave me alone" in a hideous voice I had never heard before. The men who were praying literally had to hold him so he wouldn't harm himself. The younger generation may not know what on earth I'm talking about, but the power of Satan is real, however, the power of God is the strongest and God delivered Jerry that night. It was a horrifying experience for me and I have never forgotten it.

We left for Lee Bible College in Cleveland, Tennessee in January of 1961, so Jerry could attend the second semester. My Dad paid the tuition and Henry gave us an old car. Our life in the dormitory for married people was the pits. The place was infested with roaches and we had to use a bathroom down the hall. My brother, Giles, also attended Lee and lived there with us for a couple of months. The guys went to the maintenance garage to get something to kill the bugs. There were holes in the walls and if you turned out the lights at night the roaches came running. One day they sprayed every hole in every wall of our apartment with the insecticide. The woman in the next apartment was pregnant and we heard her scream. We all went running, thinking she may be having the baby. There she was, standing on a chair. She said "all of a sudden, in broad daylight, bugs came from everywhere." Apparently, when the guys sprayed our place, the bugs just packed their bags and moved on over to her apartment.

 Jerry tried to find work but at that time there was none to be found. Times were rough and we had to pray for enough food and milk for Jeff. Due to the job situation and lack of money, we only stayed for the semester and came back home to Rochelle. Jerry decided he would just sit under the teaching of our local pastor and learn from him.

Chapter Six

My Angel

After coming home from Lee College, Jerry went to work for Del Monte Foods working long hours. In June of 1961, I became very ill and was hospitalized. I miscarried not even realizing I was pregnant. When the ordeal was over, I was relieved because I felt better and the pain was gone. It was much later that I secretly grieved over our loss. I then realized that I had a special angel in Heaven waiting for me. Some years later I sat down and wrote this poem to express how I felt about the child.

My Angel
With saddened eyes she looked at me and said "the baby's gone."
And in my heart I realized I'd never take you home.
You were quiet and oh so small, I didn't know you were there.
I wonder if you left me, thinking that I didn't care.

Why didn't you move or kick? Did I do something wrong?
I never got to hold you and sing a lullaby song.
Did God need a special angel? Were you a boy or girl?
If you had lived, would you be fair and would your hair have curls?

Would you be happy, full of life? My heart aches with pain.
In all my sorrow of losing you, I know you're Heaven's gain.
I've kept your memory tucked away in a closet of my mind
And I've learned to say to God above, not my will Lord, but Thine.

Chapter Seven

Our Growing Family

By the New Year of 1962, I realized I was expecting another baby. We had purchased a new mobile home and had two bedrooms and much more room. We were happy and waited for the arrival of this little one. He was due in mid July and by August; we still didn't have a baby. On August 3rd, I checked into the Rochelle hospital so the Doctor could induce labor. The baby was stubborn and just refused to be born no matter how hard I tried. I was exhausted, so the Doctor told the nurses to send Jerry home and they would try something else the following day. After the nurses had sent Jerry home to get some sleep, the baby decided this old world might not be so bad and he would honor us with his presence. The nurses called the Doctor back rather quickly and also called Jerry to come back to the hospital. At a few minutes till 2 a.m. on August 4, 1962, Kenneth Allen entered the world. He was a beautiful baby with dark curly hair. He was to pretty to be a boy. (Ken's stubbornness proved to be a trait that would follow him for many years. After he started school, one of his teachers sent a note home saying he was obstinate! He thought it was a compliment.) Jeff would be turning three in a couple of weeks and I felt that was a good span between the two boys. Ken never had to talk because every time he wanted something he would grunt to me and Jeff would say, "Mom, he wants a drink, or he wants a cracker." I'd ask Ken if that was what he wanted and he would nod and say "uh huh." Jeff was quite protective of his little brother. Our family was good and by this time doors were being opened and Jerry was preaching some.

I realized I was pregnant again in April of 1964. We bought a cute little house that would hold our family of soon to be five. At about the same time, Jerry was asked to pastor an Independent church outside of Rochelle. God had laid the work on my Dad's heart. Dad started out having Bible study and prayer meetings in his home. Then he began building a new church. It was here that Jerry would start his full time ministry. We started having services in the basement until we got into the new sanctuary and it was really nice. The church was named *Mission Center Tabernacle*. It was a Non-Denominational church. The spirit of God was moving in every service. People were coming from everywhere, especially on our Thursday night service. Henry was not happy with Jerry preaching somewhere other than the Church of God. He disowned him and said as far as he was concerned, Jerry was dead. Jerry's heart was broken as we went to church the next morning. In that service, God gave a message to Jerry, that if he would remain faithful, he would see his whole family saved. His oldest sister, Evelyn, started coming on Thursday nights. I don't think Henry realized that. Before long, Louise, with the younger kids, Priscilla, Peggy and Henry Jr., came with her. Henry had gone about 6 months without speaking to us and forbidding Louise to call or come by. Of course, she *would* call or come by to see the children when he was at work. One night, Henry walked into the church and found himself at an altar of prayer. Fellowship was restored and Jerry was so happy.

Just before Thanksgiving, on November 17, 1964, our only daughter, Lisa Jean was born. We were tickled pink to have a little girl. The thrill of finally having a daughter was short lived when we found she had a form of clubbed feet. Her little feet were so crooked. It would take a miracle from God and He gave us just that! People had prayed and fasted for her healing. One night during prayer, we heard the little bones snap and her feet were perfectly straight. The joy of seeing them normal was wonderful and needless to say, she got just about anything she wanted from her Daddy. He spoiled her and all she had to do was hold out her cute little feet and just name it!! Lisa was a happy little girl and very domineering of her brothers. She always wanted to call the shots and it usually got her into trouble with her Dad. Sometimes, even those cute little feet didn't help her out!

On Jerry's birthday, I had invited his parents and also mine, to come for cake and ice cream. Ken had brought some toys into the living room and piled them in the floor. I asked him to take them back to his room and he ignored me. Finally I said to Jerry, "Make him put those toys back in his room." Jerry gave the order and Ken gathered them up, and as he left the room, said with a scowl, "I'm mad." Lisa chimed in and said, "Yeah, *we're* mad, come on Ken," as she left the room and strutted down the hall in a haughty way.

They went into her bedroom, and then she looked out the door and stuck her tongue out at her Dad and called na-na-na-na-na-na! Jerry said "come here Lisa." She was just sure he was going to spank her. Sheepishly, she came to him and he told her to sit beside him and be still. She would rather get a spanking than to sit still. It was difficult for her to just sit there. She was afraid she might be missing out on something the boys were doing.

Chapter Eight

God's Will in Our Lives

Our years of Pastoral work at Mission Center were good years and we enjoyed it, but there was still something else in God's plan for us. We sold our home at auction along with most of our belongings. Jerry had scheduled some revivals during the summer. We would decide where to settle before it was time for school to start. Our summer didn't start off very well and we had three revivals canceled. That left a huge gap in our schedule. We were near Wynne, Arkansas, the town where we were both born so we rented a motel room there. Jerry went out and found a job, then cancelled the few remaining revivals. We stayed at the motel for three weeks, living in one room and eating out of a cooler. Uncle Willis Childers and Aunt Lois lived there in Wynne and we had visited them many times. Aunt Lois would come by the motel almost every day and try to get us to come for supper. We didn't want to look like free loaders and politely refused most of the time. I'll have to admit, I loved to eat at her house. She could cook better than most women I know. We soon found a house and got our few belongings out of storage and moved in. A few friends helped us set up house keeping with hand-me-down furniture, mostly *early poverty* style. With Jerry working, I also found a job and he preached revivals in that area. We stayed there for a year.

We took a trip back home to Rochelle and Jerry met with John Palmer, the new pastor of the Church of God there. They went to Decatur, IL and met with the Church of God State Overseer and Jerry was told that if a church became available, he would be appointed there. The Church of God General Assembly was in St. Louis, MO that year and we were able to attend. The official appointment was made for Jerry to pastor the Church of God in Brookport, IL. They were going to close the church if we couldn't get some excitement stirring and see a growth in attendance.

On September 9, 1970, we traveled to Brookport and moved into our first parsonage. It was a small 2 bedroom house just across the street from a stock yard. On our first night there, we were awakened to a blood curdling scream. We thought someone was being attacked in the street. As it turned out, they were prodding hogs at the stock yard. Not much sleep that night!

We were so naive then and thought everyone would love to come to our church. Well, maybe we weren't naive. People started coming and many received salvation within the first few months. The Palmers came down and conducted a revival and many were saved and joined the church. We had a lot of fun with the Palmers. They really tried to help our church grow. When they arrived at the house, their luggage was in the back seat and when they opened the car trunk, it was full of groceries. Our home church sent a *Pounding* to us. (For all the people born after the 70's, a pounding is what the old-timers called a grocery shower.) We were raised, dated, married and had our children dedicated to the Lord in that church and we were still their kids. They wanted to be of help and we were so thankful.

One day I was frying chicken for supper and was pouring the grease in a container and the pan slipped and it spilled grease all over my hand. The grease had been nearly 400 degrees just a few minutes before. It burned me really bad. I put my hand under cold running water and the Palmers started praying immediately. By the time we got supper on the table, I didn't even have a red hand. The Lord had taken the pain and redness away.

We met a couple from South Carolina named Edgar and Andrea Foster and Jerry invited them to conduct a revival three weeks before Christmas. They were young and we enjoyed their company. They were talented in music and again there were several people saved in that revival. The church began to grow in leaps and bounds. The Fosters became our close friends and we have remained friends through the years.

During that revival as Christmas was approaching, we didn't have any extra money for toys for the kids. They had as usual, made their wish list and had given it to me. As I looked over the list, even though it was a short list, I knew there was no way we could buy these things. Jerry asked me to talk to them and explain that if we waited until after Christmas, things would be on sale. We might be able to get one thing on the list for each of them. I just couldn't do that. We had always worked a secular job and made enough money to provide them with a fairly good Christmas. Why would God make them do without now that their parents were doing His work? I totaled up the cost of the simple list of toys. It would take at least $100.00 to provide for the three of them and buy the makings for a Christmas turkey dinner. I began to pray. I knew that $100.00 was a lot of money back then, but, not a lot for God and all I could do was trust Him. In my mind, I had figured out several ways in which the Lord could meet my need. I knew we could call our folks and they would send money to help us out, but I was not going to do that. Every day, I would go to the bathroom to pray, (the only private place in the house.) We had always been faithful to God in tithing and giving…..sometimes giving all we had to a worthy cause or needy family. I felt that I must trust God!

The Fosters were still there and one day I had fixed lunch and they were in the kitchen with Jerry and me. The subject of Christmas gifts came up and Jerry asked me if I had said anything to the kids yet. I began to tell about praying for the $100 and added that I believed my prayer would be answered in time. While I was speaking, there was a knock on the door and I finished my sentence before I went to answer it. Standing on our porch were two men, Joe Kickasola and his father. We barely knew them. I invited them in and they stepped inside. As he was pulling out his wallet, Joe said "we don't have much time; I just wanted to stop by and give you and Brother Holt a little Christmas gift." He simply reached in without counting and grabbed a handful of bills and handed them to me, all crumpled up. I smoothed out five, twenty dollar bills and let out a squeal of joy. Jerry and the Fosters came rushing in, to see what the noise was about. Jerry told Joe that I had been praying for that exact amount to help us through Christmas. Joe's dad, Mr. Luke, gave me a big toothless smile and said, I'd like to get in on this blessing and he handed me a ten dollar bill. Right there before my eyes was more money than I had asked for. KJV Luke 6:38 says, "Give, and it shall be given unto you, good measure, pressed down, and shaken together, and running over, shall men give to your bosom. For with the same measure that ye mete withal it shall be measured to you again." When God supplies, He even gives extra and it had come from where I had least expected. We were able to get everything on the "list" that year.

Our district pastor was Jim Jones and he was Pastor of the Church of God in Harrisburg, Illinois. Jerry's first impression of Jim wasn't anything to "write home about." I found his wife, Gwen, to be very outgoing and friendly. She was a good organist and also a good hostess. We became great friends and spent a lot of time together.

Jerry and Jim served on the same State Boards and we made several trips to the State Office together. Gwen and I would shop while the men got to sit in a stuffy meeting all day.

The Joneses were people we could put our confidence in and it didn't go any farther. We are close friends still. They have moved to Orlando, Florida and even though we don't get to see them as often as we'd like to, distance does not change friendships.

Chapter Nine

The Shock!

Within a couple of years, we had outgrown our church building and needed to build a new sanctuary. Jerry talked to my Dad, who had been a builder for years. A plan was decided on. The church men wanted to build the building themselves to save money. In March of 1973, Dad came to oversee the digging of the footing and getting the framework up. By July the work was nearly completed. I had not been feeling well and went to the Doctor for a checkup and was shocked out of my mind. He told me that by Christmas I would have another baby. I had been told by the same Doctor that I probably would not have any more children, due to some female problems I had been having for five to six years. During this time, Jerry had a lot on his mind and I wasn't going to bother him with what I thought was my *"not so terrific news."* After all, Lisa was nearly nine and we hadn't had diapers and baby bottles in our house for years!

With the church being built by donated help, after a few months, the helpers were few and far between. The building was nearly finished and Jerry was anxious to keep things going. Finally, *two days after* I went to the Doctor, he stopped on his way out the door to work and asked what the Doctor had said. I told him to sit down and we would talk about it. He refused to sit, saying he was in a hurry. I urged him to sit down, but he didn't have time. I just blurted out, "I'm pregnant." *Then* he sat down and didn't say a word or move for two hours. He was absolutely speechless! It was just that he too, realized that Lisa was almost 9 years old and would be going on 10 when this baby would be born. The shock wore off soon and we took things in stride. One morning we were all at the breakfast table and Lisa told her Dad that she had decided what she wanted for Christmas. Now get this, it was just July and she was already making her Christmas list! Since we didn't have health insurance to pay for this baby, Jerry said to her, "your Mother went last week and picked out a Christmas gift for all of us." She was thrilled and said "oh Dad, give us a hint!" He said, "Well, it's wet most of the time." She squealed out "a swimming pool!" Jerry's teenage brother was visiting us and he asked "oh no, are you going to have another kid?" I smiled and told him "yes, we were having a Christmas baby." They didn't believe us. Lisa said "Mom stop teasing us and tell us what we're getting for Christmas." I assured them that we were telling the truth and asked them not to tell anyone at church just yet. The very next Sunday morning, Lisa pleaded, "Mom, let me tell about the baby. I just can't keep it quiet any longer." I gave her permission to share our news.

She stood at the door of the church and shook hands with people as they came in and said, "guess what, my Mom's gonna have a baby!!" As it turned out, no one believed her!

Well, Christmas came and went and we didn't have a baby. I began to wonder if this child would be as stubborn as Ken had been. Finally after induction of labor on January 22, 1974, we welcomed Jeremy Wade into our family. He had black hair and of course brown eyes and was beautiful. His hair was long and straight. He looked like a little Eskimo child. When the other three were born we were just kids ourselves, now, we had grown up. We really enjoyed raising him. He was a quiet child and a Daddy's boy. I guess he didn't know what to think about his noisy siblings and decided to be quiet. Oh course, Lisa decided to boss him as well. He turned our life up-side down and brought a lot of laughter and joy to the family.

We had been in the new building at Brookport for about 2 years, when the State Overseer asked Jerry to accept the pastorate of the Indian Trail Church of God in Aurora, IL. We agreed and when Jerry announced his resignation, grown men cried. We had made many good friends in those 5 years and most of our congregation had come to salvation under Jerry's ministry. It was a sad time for us, yet an exciting time. However, we felt it was the best thing for us. The thought of moving to a large city was exciting and we would be just an hour from our home town. Aurora, with its thousands seemed huge compared to Brookport with its population of nine hundred people. The next three years would bring good memories and also some of the worst times we had ever gone through. The church in Aurora was in the process of selling their parsonage. Since it had not sold yet, we didn't unpack everything. It did sell and we had to move again in 3 months. We were able to buy a beautiful split level home. It was the nicest place we had ever lived. Since the house was so much larger than the previous one had been, the Church Council gave us a generous allotment for furniture and we were able to decorate it the way we wanted to.

I had planned an Open House so everyone could come and see the new parsonage with the new furniture. I had been cleaning and shining, getting everything ready. One night Jeremy seemed to be feverish and came and got in bed with Jerry and me. I got up to get the Bayer children's aspirin and gave him one. I thought I had put the lid on tight, but evidently didn't. The next morning after making the bed, I never went back to our bedroom. I worked on the lower level of the house most of the day. Jeremy had napped in the den on the sofa and woke up about supper time. I was taking rolls out of the oven and he stood in the doorway and said "yum Mama, nico (candy) good," as he opened his mouth to show the remains of pink baby aspirin. I was so shook up, I touched the hot oven, burned my hand and rolls went rolling all over the kitchen floor. Jeremy squealed out in laughter.

I thought, "Oh my Lord, he is out of his head from the medicine!" I ran for the bedroom to get the aspirin bottle. It was empty and I found one aspirin on the floor. The night before, I had opened a new bottle and had given him only one out of it. He had gone into the bedroom without me seeing him and had chewed and swallowed 34 aspirins! I ran downstairs and told Jerry. We immediately took him to the hospital and they gave him something to make him vomit. Within 30 minutes he had vomited all of them. The blood tests showed no damage and there was not enough aspirin in the blood stream to hurt him. We took him home and thanked God that he wasn't injured from the ordeal.

Just watching him grow brought us a lot of joy. It was here he learned to ride a bicycle. Henry had bought him a used little bike with 12 inch wheels and the tires were molded rubber and had big chunks in them. Jeff took a knife or something and smoothed out the tires so it would not ride so bumpy. Jeremy would put on a little helmet and ride as fast as he could go. Hum, I wonder where he got that gene for speed.

Chapter Ten

Cheating Death

On May 13, 1976, Jerry was having chest pain. I finally convinced him to go to the ER. Within minutes the Doctor said they were moving him to the fifth (I believe) floor. I didn't know it was the Cardiac Care floor. I was asked to wait in a waiting area and they would let me know when I could go in and see him. I heard a "code blue" called and nurses started scurrying everywhere. I had no idea what was happening. Since Jerry was only 35 years old I figured he probably had indigestion. The hospital chaplain approached me and asked "are you Mrs. Holt?" I said "yes." He said "don't be upset, everything is okay now. Would you please come with me?" I still didn't realize what was happening.

He took me to the Coronary Care unit and there lay Jerry. He had gone bald at an early age and had started wearing a wig. I noticed immediately that his wig had been removed and he was wet with heavy sweat. I saw his Doctor and a surgeon standing in the hall and Jerry started to beg me, "Please don't sign any papers." I wondered what was really going on. As it turned out, he had suffered Cardiac arrest during a heart attack. They were waiting to put a pacemaker in his chest, but he would not sign for the surgery. In a weak voice Jerry shared with me what he had just seen while he was technically dead. It was an incredible story and he said, "Betty I love you and the kids, but the place I have just seen is so beautiful, I want to go there." After hearing the Doctor say, "I think we have lost him" Jerry got a glimpse of the *other side*. As he passed through darkness, he came into a beautiful light and there he saw throngs of people waving and cheering him home. He said he was so excited and started to run toward this beautiful place but then suddenly, he heard a voice boom, "not now." He opened his eyes and saw a little nurse about to pound him in the chest. She thought she had seen a heart beat on the monitor and wanted to make sure she completely revived him. He had already been pounded on and shocked.

I saw the heart monitor tape piled in the floor and up across his bed and down the other side and piled in the floor, without one heart beat on it. His heart had been stopped that long. It was difficult to tell the Doctors that I wouldn't sign for the surgery. They were very upset with me and tried to scare me by saying, if it ever happened again, away from the hospital, there would not be time to save him.

This was really a scary thought for me, but I knew that God had spared him for a reason. Later tests would show an abnormality in his heart. Immediately after the heart attack, Jerry was depressed and discouraged. The church seemed to be at a spiritual standstill. We had been in Aurora for just over 9 months and there had been no conversions. Jerry didn't feel well most of the time and questioned in his mind if he was in God's will. Our state Camp Meeting was convening in Benton, Illinois and he approached the Overseer about being assigned to another church. One was offered and it happened to be nearby. One afternoon after the morning service of Camp Meeting, we drove to the nearby town to look over the property. Although we were praying, nothing spoke to our hearts. That evening, Jerry felt the Lord speak and told him to go back home to Aurora and he would be blessed. On the following Sunday, to our amazement, 29 new adults came walking in the church and sat in the pews. Jerry ministered under a great anointing that morning and every one of those new people came to the altar to give their heart to God. As it turned out, they were all related and owned their own business. They were in Aurora on a special job and were living at a nearby Holiday Inn. Their job lasted several weeks and they became regular attendees while they were in town. They had never experienced salvation before. God was blessing and our church began to grow.

The doctors had finally set up an appointment for him to go to Mayo Clinic in Rochester, MN., The night before we were to leave, Jerry preached in lots of pain. I was the organist for the church and usually sat on the platform during his message to be available for the invitational. All of a sudden, it felt that my hair would stand straight up and I saw a new step in Jerry's walk and movement. There was rejoicing in the pews because everyone felt that the healing had taken place. We went on to Mayo and stayed there for a week and through test after test, the Doctors could not find the problem that had showed on the video tape a few months earlier. Again, God had done a great work.

Chapter Eleven

Happy Times/Sad times

After almost three years in Aurora, at the request of the State Overseer, Jerry consented to pastor the Church of God in Logan, IL I did not want to make this move. I loved where we were living and I loved the church people. We had made some long lasting friends in those three years. We still keep in touch with some of them today. Jeff had attended one year and one semester at Lee College and had dropped out to work and make some money before going back. He had a good job and some people from the church said he could live with them and continue to work until we got settled in at our new church in Logan.

We packed our things and made the move in April of 1978. Since our parsonage would not be ready until the following week end, we decided to go on and visit my parents, who by this time had retired in Arkansas. We got to Paducah, KY late that Friday night and stayed in a motel before going on to see Mom and Dad. The next morning over breakfast, the kids and especially Jeremy, wanted to go to Brookport and visit with Bob and Ethel Henley. They had been like God parents to Jeremy and close friends of ours. We drove over and they were glad to see us. Of course a fishing trip was soon planned by Bob and Jerry. As they were leaving, Ken and the Henley's son Eugene were horsing around in the yard and told the men they were going fishing too. Jerry started scuffling around with them, just laughing and goofing off. Both boys lunged at Jerry and he lost his balance and fell, with both boys on top of him. They were still laughing when they heard Jeremy cry out. They discovered that he had just run up behind Jerry, wanting to join in the fun. The two boys and Jerry were all three on top of Jeremy's leg. It was a bad break. He spent 10 days in traction and then was put in a body cast for the next 10 weeks. The hospital was about 70 miles from where our home was to be and Jerry and I took turns staying day and night with him.

With Jeff still living in Aurora, Ken and Lisa helped me get the boxes unpacked and the house "put together." About eight weeks later, Jeff decided to join us. He had a car accident on the way to our house. Thank God he wasn't injured. Ken was riding a bicycle and went over the handlebars and we made a trip to the ER for stitches on his lip and chin. Jokingly, Jerry told me to keep Lisa in the house for the rest of the summer for fear something would happen to her. God was probably trying to tell us, that He had not favored this move. We had taken about enough. It was a miserable summer, and we began to pray for God to show us His perfect will.

My oldest brother, Dewey, had planned a 65th surprise birthday party for my Dad. We went to the event with Jeremy in the cast. He lay on pillows in the back seat of the car. The party was fun and a great surprise to Dad. All his children were there along with his siblings. We "roasted" him and some very funny stories were told that day. I did not realize that he would only live, exactly nine more months.

Brother James Qualls, who was at the Brookport church, had, at one time, been the pastor in Logan. He called Jerry and asked if we would consider coming back to Brookport and he would like to return to Logan. Everything was worked out with the State Officials. In October of 1978, we moved from Logan and back to Brookport for the second time. Our kids were happy and it felt like we were home again. Jeff had gone back to college by this time. A few days after we had moved back to Brookport, he called and told us he had found the "love of his life." He had known her since he started his freshman year at college. She sang with the Ladies of Lee choir and Jeff was the bass guitar player for them. Her name was Sherle Marie Groover and she was from Jesup, GA. Yes, we thought she was a peach. Jeff brought her home to meet us over their New Year's break and we had 6-8 inches of snow. I don't think she had ever seen that much snow on the ground. We enjoyed Sherle's visit with us and by the time they went back to college, we also, had fallen in love with her.

Just the next month after meeting Sherle, I received a terrible telephone call. It was a sad day on February 22, 1979 when my Dad had a heart attack and died on the spot. Our church family stood beside us during this sad time. Some of the church people drove to Arkansas to the funeral. I had always felt closeness to my Dad. He had a great knowledge of the Bible. I had sat under his teaching in church for many years. He had been there for Jerry and me all through the years, never condemning or butting in. He had a great interest in Jerry's ministry. There had been times when Dad stood beside us when it seemed no one else understood.

I don't ever remember hearing him call me Betty. Mom had picked out the name of Betty and Dad liked the name Jean, so they named me Betty Jean. Dad always called me Betjean. No one else ever called me that and I liked it that way. Even at the writing of this, I still miss him greatly. Jerry also grieved at Dad's passing. He had lost a confidant and good friend.

Jeff and Sherle got married on July 27, 1979. We made the trip to Jesup, Georgia for the wedding. I had a rehearsal dinner to get together and our friends, Vern and Hazel Giltner and their girls drove their car down with us to lend a helping hand. The extra help from the Giltners certainly was a blessing. The dinner went off without a hitch. We served a sit down meal of ham with all the trimmings. Although three of our children married away from Brookport, Vern and Hazel attended every wedding.

It was the first time we had ever met Sherle's family. They were all very nice to us. The wedding was very beautiful. After the happy couple left on their honeymoon to Jekyll Island, GA, we headed for home, taking the time to sight see on the way back.

Chapter Twelve

Tragedy

There were times when I have wondered if God really knew what was going on in my life. The next few years would bring a lot of pain, sorrow and death. My brother, Dewey, had done very well through the years and owned his own business, where they mixed chemicals and made rubber. He had bought a new building to use as a warehouse. There was a problem of some kind and Dewey climbed a ladder and fell off. His son, Tim, found him. I asked Tim, to refresh my memory of exactly what happened and he gave me the following report and permission to use his own words.

Tim said, "The new building had a burst water pipe from a freeze that winter. Dad was on an extension ladder about 20 feet up. He had a bad back. I can remember times when he would be sitting at his desk and reach for a pencil when his back would catch and he would double over in pain. While I don't have any direct proof, I think that's what happened on the ladder. He was awake when I found him. He was in a bathroom washing his face. He had, as I recall, 3 skull fractures that almost met as one long one all the way around his skull. He lost consciousness when I was driving him to the hospital. They did surgery, but there was a bleeder they couldn't reach."

My brother went to be with the Lord on March 13, 1981. It was so tragic. He had too much going for him, to be taken in the prime of his life. He was only 47 years old. He left behind his wife Ruby and two grown sons, Steve and Tim. We grieved, but I know he would not come back if he had the chance. I often wondered just why God allowed something like this to happen. There is an old song that says "we'll understand it better, by and by." I have to believe that.

We thought we had taken all we could handle as a family, but just 2 and 1/2 months later, my sister gave up in her battle with cancer. She was diagnosed with breast cancer in 1978 and had surgery. It was touch and go for the next couple of years and then things went downhill. On May 27, 1981 she went to be with the Lord leaving behind 4 daughters. The three youngest were ages 6 through 15 and the oldest was married. Again we were saddened, but knew she was now at home. Life's lessons are hard to learn, and I learned that healing doesn't always come in this life.

I know that her body is whole again and she is no longer in pain. Although there were eight years between us in age, we had gotten close after I had married. I really felt that I had lost not only a sister, but a good friend.

Chapter Thirteen

My Gains and My Loses

Don and his wife, Marilyn took Bobbie's daughter, Andrea, age 15, to live with them. Jerry and I took Stephanie age 6 and Connie age 13, to live with us. It was quite a challenge to have two more children in the house. With Bobbie being divorced, the girls had been raised in an all female house. They thought they could continue in their usual habits of bathing and lying around watching TV, in their night gowns without underpants on. We told them they had to wear robes over their gowns and underwear was to be worn anytime they were out of their bedroom. Little Stephanie just could not understand. She said "my Mommy told me I need to air my boodie every night after my bath!" Well, we let her air that boodie as long as she stayed in her bedroom!

During the time we lived in Aurora, Illinois, I became good friends with a woman in our church named Judy Harrington. She and her husband, Ted had three children about the ages of ours. Ted worked for the railroad. Judy and I were about as different as night and day, but we became best friends. I loved her like a sister. As a foursome, we camped together, played games, went places together and spent time in each other's home. Some years had passed and we had moved on to a church in DeKalb Illinois. We heard from the Harringtons and found that they had dropped out of church so we invited them to come and attend with us. They started attending and the friendship was renewed. One New Year's Eve, I invited them to come and see the New Year in with us. We played games and snacked all night until 6:00 am. We thought we might need to get some sleep so we all went to bed. At 9:00 am, I awoke to the smell of coffee and got up to find Judy in the kitchen. She could not sleep any longer and was ready to face the New Year. We sat and had coffee together talking until the men woke up.

Judy was elected as our church clerk. She was very efficient and did her job well. Jerry usually got paid on Sunday and over the years; before going home after the services, he would have to ask former clerks if his paycheck was ready. Most of the time it had not been written and he would stand and wait for the clerk to get it done. This made Jerry feel very uncomfortable. Judy never made him feel that way.

At some point on Sunday morning, she would slip in his office (while he was shaking hands with people coming in) and place on his desk a sealed envelope containing his paycheck. He never had to mention or remind her that it was payday.

In January of 1985 our hearts were crushed when she gave us the word that the Doctor's had found cancer. She resigned her position saying that she would not have the time to do the job properly with all the tests she would be going through. The following months were sad as I watched her body fade into a shell. Her spirits were still high and she would joke at her new skinny body. I laughed along with her, but my heart was aching inside. She was in and out of the hospital many times that year and was hospitalized as Christmas was approaching. Judy begged to go home for the holiday. The Doctor let her go home for just a few days. We visited her the day after Christmas. Her son, Doug, had given her three beautiful dresses. They were all too big for her new size, but I think he was in denial and hoped she would recover to wear them. She was so proud of them and told me that she had decided to be buried in the cream colored one. It was the prettiest of all. We talked of all the good times we'd had together. My heart was breaking, but I tried to keep the conversation cheerful. Her voice was weak as she began telling me some things she wanted done. Even in her weakened state, she was thinking of her kids and Ted. She asked if we would see to it, that they would be okay.

She went back into the hospital the next day. Judy passed away the first week in January of 1986 about a year after the cancer diagnoses was made. I have never had a better friend and still remember the good times we had together. Heaven is sweeter because she is there.

It was in DeKalb where Lisa found the love of her life. His name was Jackie Frank Summers, Jr. He wanted to be called Jack. Lisa asked if she could invite him to Sunday dinner and I agreed. At Lisa's request, we put a really good meal on the table to impress this young man. Our church people would often bring garden vegetables to the house and that day I had washed them good and made a beautiful salad. We were all sitting at the dining table and eight year old Jeremy asked loudly, "Mom is this green thing in my salad, a worm?" I said "Jeremy there is *not* a worm in your salad." He replied, "Well, whatever it is, it's crawling." Sure enough it was a tiny green worm. Lisa was about to serve Jack some salad and of course he politely refused. She was sure he would never come back. Well he did many times and proposed to her that following April.

The wedding was set for August 20, 1983. Lisa and I were in a frenzy the next few weeks getting everything planned and ordered. Jack had taken a vacation to Denver, CO and bought her a beautiful blown glass figurine in the shape of a heart with love birds. He gave it to her when he returned and proposed. We were trying to find just the right thing for the top of the wedding cake. We finally decided to use the blown glass figurine. The morning of her wedding day, I carefully put it in my car to drop off at the reception hall for my cousin, Vickie, who had baked the cake.

I carefully laid it in the front seat. My passenger door was not closed well and as I reached over to give it another slam, my elbow hit the figurine. It broke in three pieces. I drove on to the reception hall and was bawling my eyes out. The ladies there, told me to go home and relax, they would see to it that everything would turn out fine. That evening I went to the ceremony with red eyes, but that is usually expected for the Mother of the Bride. Lisa and Jack had asked Jeff to perform the ceremony and I cried again as I watched Jerry walk his only daughter down the aisle. I hadn't told Lisa about breaking the love birds, because I didn't want to spoil her day. Sure enough after the ceremony we all gathered in the reception hall and there it sat atop the cake. It was glistening! After the newly-weds returned from their honeymoon, they came over to get the remainder of Lisa's things. I had put the figurine in a box to protect it. As I was telling her about breaking it and crying and crying she was opening the box to check it out. Suddenly, she lost her grasp and the love birds fell on the carpeted floor and broke into a million pieces. It was so sad, but then we began to laugh. She saved the broken glass for several years before throwing it away.

We had been having a problem with my niece, Connie, who was sixteen years old at that time. She just could not fit in to our lifestyle. My sister had been mostly bedfast for a long time. For over a year the girls had practically raised themselves and took care of their Mother. Even though Connie had been with us for three years, she just would not conform to living in a Pastor's home. We told her she would have to leave and in June of 1984 she and Stephanie went to live with Andrea at Don's house. We decided to give Stephanie a choice to stay or go with her sister. She didn't want to be separated from Connie and she chose to go with her. It proved to be a decision we would live to regret in later years. Connie later married after she graduated from High School and had a daughter and a son. Her health had been a problem most of her life and she passed away at the age of 37 years old.

With Jeff being married four years, Lisa newly married, Connie and Stephanie gone, the house seemed empty. Ken had been seeing a girl named Deborah McKinney, but it seemed to be an on again, off again relationship. He was 22 years old and didn't seem to have any intentions of getting married. As it turned out, Debbie and her family had been members of our church in Aurora. She had a story similar to mine and even as a young girl had claimed Ken for her husband. Time would tell.

Just before our 25th wedding anniversary both married couples told us we would be grandparents in the fall. We were thrilled and it looked like the babies would be born pretty near the same time.

Lisa delivered first. Ryan Andrew Summers was born September 18, 1984. He weighed a little over 7 pounds. He was a cute baby with lots of hair. We got to watch through the window while the nurse cleaned him up and got him dressed. What a good feeling! Grandparents at last!

A couple of weeks after Ryan was born; Jerry's Mom was staying with us for a few days. Henry had already passed away. Louise was in the living room rocking the baby. Lisa and I were in the kitchen. Suddenly we heard the most beautiful singing. It was a great grandmother singing a beautiful hymn to her first great grandchild. I had never heard her sing before that. It showed me where Jerry got his pretty singing voice.

Sherle had been waiting patiently and her tummy grew larger. I thought she would have a baby as stubborn as its Uncle Ken. Finally, on October 13, 1984, Brandon Thomas Holt entered this world weighing in at 10 pounds and 7 ounces. Sherle had to have a C-section and there were complications and both she and the baby were in distress. Brandon was the largest baby in the nursery and was the only one in an incubator. He was almost a month younger than Ryan and was bigger already. We went to the hospital in Decatur, IL to see them and the nurse brought the baby out for Sherle to feed. Jerry and I laughed at the little bundle. He was so husky and looked like a miniature Sumo Wrestler. Jeff wanted to feed him and that child inhaled 4 ounces of formula at his first feeding. We knew then this was going to be a big boy. It was the best time of my life during the next couple of years. It was such a joy to see the babies crawling around and playing, then toddling around, sharing then fighting over toys, attention or whatever. The boys were as different as day and night. Brandon was a big husky voiced boy and Ryan thin and fair. They became buddies at an early age. Could things get any better? Life was good!

Ken and Debbie's romance had taken a turn for the worse and they had been broken up for a few weeks. One day I was vacuuming in the downstairs den and suddenly felt that my breath had been punched out of me. I felt the Lord say, "Ken will marry Debbie." I wondered where that came from. I had not even had them on my mind at that time. The voice proved to be right. Debbie was a very pretty girl and had long golden blond hair. She became a regular fixture around our house and we became good friends. One day she asked me if I would give her a home permanent. I said I would and told her to buy one for color treated hair. She looked at me funny and asked "why"? I tried to explain to her that anyone who colored or bleached their hair needed that type of perm so it would curl well and be gentle. She said "I don't color my hair or bleach it." I don't know if my face was as red as I felt it was, but I was really embarrassed. Her hair was a beautiful natural blond. She has enjoyed bringing this up through the years to get back at me! We have good laugh.

At Christmas time in 1985, I asked Ken what he had bought Debbie for Christmas and he replied "purple socks." Well, purple *was* her favorite color, but I told him he needed to get her something more or better than just a pair of socks. He was firm and said, "No, I'm all finished shopping." Well we found out later that he had bought an engagement ring. He took it to a nice store downtown DeKalb, purchased the socks and put the ring in the toe of one of them, before having the box wrapped. Can you imagine her surprise when she opened her gift and he slipped down on one knee as she found the ring? There in our living room, he proposed. What a romantic thing for him to do. But after all, he was twenty-three years old and had plenty of time to think of something romantic! They were married on April 19, 1986. Ken had asked Jerry to conduct the ceremony. It was a beautiful wedding.

Once Ken had pulled a stunt when he was around 6-7 and he ran away from home. I think he was mad at me for something. Anyway, it was suppertime and he was no where to be found! We searched and searched for him and was about to call the police and then go searching door to door. About that time Jeff and my niece, Risa, found him walking home. He must have gotten over his madness toward me and had been playing with a neighbor kid down the street. His Daddy used a belt on him and said "don't you ever do that again."

We had always teased Ken by saying he would never marry and leave home, but would be an old bachelor. Ken would reply that he was afraid to leave and get married because he might get a belting again! That boy!

In September of 1986 Jerry resigned our church at DeKalb and we moved into a rented house in Creston, IL. Lisa was pregnant again and the baby was due in October. Jerry was preaching revivals and traveling full time and I had started a job with Amoco as a dispatcher. I had called her at noon one day and she said she wasn't feeling well. No labor pains, just a lot of pressure. After work I went by their apartment to pick up Ryan and take him home with me, thinking she would deliver that night. Jack took her to the hospital and as I was getting Ryan ready for bed, I called to see how far she had progressed. Jack said her pains were strong, but it would probably be a while, but he would call no matter what time of night she delivered. I had just gone to bed when the phone rang and it was Lisa. I thought, oh my, there is a problem or she is afraid or she just wants to talk to her Mom to calm her mind. She said "hello Grandma." Well, I was already a Grandma so it didn't register. She said "Grandma, you have a new grandson!" I was thrilled. She had given birth and was already sitting up in bed and talking to me! That Girl!!

It was October 8, 1986, when Kyle Adam entered the world at over 9 pounds. He was a beautiful baby. He grew to be nearly as big as Ryan in just two years. He was Ryan's shadow. Ryan was thin and Kyle, just the opposite with a husky build. They were inseparable and became great buddies. They were so much alike in their ways. Even today, I have a hard time telling them apart when I see them at a distance or hear their voice on the phone.

In June of 1987 we moved back to Brookport so Jerry could evangelize in several states and be at home in only 5-6 hours instead of 11-12. We had another miracle from God. Someone had bought us a very nice 28 foot motor home for Jerry to travel in. Jeremy had started 8th grade and again we stayed at home so he could stay in school. On a few occasions Jeremy and I drove to meet Jerry on the weekend. This way we were able to spend some time with him and be in the church services.

Sherle was expecting another baby and we knew the day she would deliver, because she was having another C-section. During a revival I was able to attend with Jerry, we were called and told that Sherle had given birth to another son. It was great news even though by then I was wondering if we would ever get a granddaughter.

From my Heart and Soul

Nicholas Jordan entered the world on June 8, 1988. We would not get to see him until August. He was a beautiful baby and had a mind of his own. Actually he was to pretty to be a boy. He had beautiful blonde curly hair. Being the youngest of the 4 grandsons, he pretty much got his way. Of course in a couple of years, they would trick him into doing things that would get him in big trouble. Nick was gullible enough to do them and yes he got in trouble. They laughed at him, out of my sight, of course.

Since the boys lived several hundred miles apart there wasn't a good chance for them to bond as cousins. After they had gotten to be three through six years old, we tried to have the four of them come every summer for a week or two. We didn't have a pool, so I had bought a big sprinkler for them to play in during those hot days. On one visit, I had dressed them all so I could run some errands in town. Their orders were to wait on the deck and I would be out in a few minutes. When

I went outside, Ryan, Brandon and Kyle were soaking wet. Nicholas was standing dry and smiling big. The older boys said they had walked out in the yard and Nicholas had turned the sprinkler on and soaked them. When I asked Nick if that was true, he grinned and said "yes ma'am." I took the fly swatter (bought for spanking purposes) and spanked him, redressed the other three and we headed out. Later, after we got back home, the other three confessed. They had stood at the sprinkler and *told* Nick to turn the water on. Of course, he did as he was told. Well, then it was time for the other boys to line up and get their spanking. I attribute several of my gray hairs to those visits! Now that they are grown up, I must admit, I would like to recall some of those days. We enjoyed our time with the four of them together.

When we moved back to Brookport, in 1987, we bought an old house and discovered it had termite damage and we needed a new front porch. The old porch had been torn off and a friend, Leon Brannan had come to help Jerry build a new one. It was in late September, 1988, and one morning when Jerry came to the table for breakfast, I scolded him for trimming his moustache crooked. I told him it was all lopsided. He tried to speak to me and I knew then that something was wrong. I hurriedly called Leon and told him not to come that day because Jerry was sick. We went to the ER and after tests were done, I was told that he had suffered a stroke. I had to cancel several weeks of revivals because he had a difficult time speaking. Leon and his son came anyway and finished the porch. After a few weeks, Jerry had mended, and went to work for a friend at his construction company. His body had mended, but he still had a hard time with some of his speech.

Chapter Fourteen

My Mother-in-Law, my Friend

As I look back on my life, I can say I was blessed with a wonderful Mother-in-law. Most girls complain about that "other woman" in their husband's life. Louise became one of my closest friends. I know she loved me as her own child. There are many times I would bear my soul to her and I believe she kept it in her heart. She came from a nice home and her mother was a nurse. (Her mother, Irene Wright was a very religious woman and was the first to realize that God had His hand on Jerry's life.) In fact, she told Louise that God was going to make a preacher out of him. Louise always lived in town and was strictly female. When she married Henry, he took her to his folks' home to live (like many did back then.) They lived out in the boonies and Henry had 4 younger brothers. They all worked in the fields trying to make a living so the job of chief cook and bottle washer went to Louise. It was a hard life for her but she survived!

In late November after Jerry's stroke, we got a call that Louise was not doing well and we needed to come. We made the trip to Rochelle and found Louise in the hospital and had several things wrong. We stayed a few days and she seemed to remain about the same, so we went back home to get Jeremy back in school. After a couple of weeks we got another call to come quickly. She would not last the night. Jerry was out on a job and I had to go searching for him. He came home and cleaned up while I packed clothes. We got on the road and drove quickly, dreading what we would find. Jerry had me drive the last several miles so he could rest. Just as we got near the Rochelle exit, I had turned the radio dial to get some gospel music and there I heard Louise's favorite song playing. It was "Peace Peace Wonderful Peace." I had a strange feeling come over me and I felt we would not get there before she passed away. As we drove up to the hospital there stood Ken and someone else, I can't remember who. I knew then that we were too late. They said she had passed away quietly about 10 minutes before we arrived. I believe she was carried away by the angels, maybe even on the airways of that song she loved so much.

It was December 1988, just a few days before Christmas and I had lost a wonderful friend. I still miss her and at times wish I could just sit and talk to her for a bit.

I have always hoped that I would be as good a Mother-in-law to the girls my sons married, as Louise was to me.

It had been many years since she passed away and I had been doing ancestry research for some time. I found that Louise's parents divorced when she was just one year old. I knew her parents were divorced, but I didn't realize she had been so young. My heart was saddened to learn that. I tried to imagine what her life was like without a Father there for her. Her Dad was alive, but there was not closeness between them. He had remarried soon after the divorce and his new wife was not friendly with all of Grandpa's children. After Louise had been married several years, the closeness was restored.

Chapter Fifteen

The Beginning of Empty Nest Syndrome

The following spring, the Pastor's Council of the Brookport Church of God, approached Jerry about becoming pastor again. The present pastor had resigned and was leaving. Jerry told them "no," and still they persisted. After much prayer Jerry consented to have his name submitted for the pastoral vote. The vote was taken and Jerry received nearly a 100 per cent vote. This would be our third time here in this position. I think to receive that percentage of a vote after two former stays, speaks well of Jerry. The people had confidence in him and there were many things that needed "fixing" to get the church back on solid ground.

We bought a new home outside of town and settled in. Jeremy was a sophomore in High School by then and was enjoying football and baseball. I, who had never attended a football game since my own high school years was his number one fan. I didn't know what was going on most of the time, but I yelled and cheered anyway. Sometimes I cheered at the wrong time! Jeremy was a good player and gave everything he had to the game. I shuttered when I heard the helmets crash against each other. Not long after the season started in his sophomore year, I watched as he made a play and broke a bone in his hand.

He just kept playing and when he went to the sidelines, the strength coach taped him up. After the game he wanted to ride the bus back to the school. We told the coach that we would meet them at the school and take him to the ER ourselves. The Doctor on call told us Jeremy would need to see a bone specialist. Not only was the bone broken, but it had been jammed pretty bad due to his continued playing. The bone was set and his hand and arm put in a cast. After a few weeks, he was right back out there giving it all he had!

From my Heart and Soul

Jeremy was the only one of our children who was able to attend school with the same friends for five straight years. We had moved many times in the ministry and Lisa and the older boys attended several schools. Hindsight is so clear. We should have stuck longer in one place. By the end of his senior year, he had excelled in football and baseball. I saved all the newspaper clippings about the local games. Finally the day came for him to graduate. His graduation was a joyous occasion. His brothers and sister and their families came home for the event.

The gymnasium was packed that night and cameras were flashing everywhere. When they called his name, I was proud.

The other three had graduated, but this was different. Our child rearing days were about over. Jeremy was near manhood and I knew his time with us would be limited. College was ahead in just a couple of short months. I didn't know how I would deal with the empty nest syndrome. The day came for him to leave for Cleveland Tennessee to attend Lee University and of course his Dad and I went along to help him get settled in. My heart was heavy as we started out. Jeremy followed us in his car. We stopped at a rest area and Jerry suggested I ride the remainder of the way with Jeremy in case we got separated. I knew the way to Cleveland and Jeremy had never driven it alone. He and I had a fun ride and shared a few laughs along the way. It got my mind off what was soon to come.

When we got there and saw his room, I almost cried. Summer camp had better rooms. I could not believe my eyes and thought "they are charging us for **this**??" When Jerry and I headed for home, my heart was so full. I knew if I let go, the tears would be flooding down and I would probably make Jerry cry too. He was driving and I didn't want that to happen. I didn't know that he was on the same brink of tears as I was.

After the first semester, Jeremy was able to move to another dorm. I was glad, because during the following semester, that dorm burned. An arsonist started the fire in a room on the first floor, just beneath Jeremy's old room. He was a very sound sleeper and may not have awakened if he had still been living there. No one was killed in the fire and the arsonist was eventually caught.

The weeks and months that would follow his leaving for college, was a sad time in our home. We missed our last born so much. The empty nest causes the heart to ache, but time does heal. At this writing, Jeremy has never married and even now when he comes home and goes out to a movie or somewhere with friends, his Dad will say "wonder what time he's coming home." Those parenting feelings never leave us.

Chapter Sixteen

Grandson Number Five

We were in our sixth year, on our third time at Brookport. The church was doing very well. Jerry had heard of a lady minister from Georgia whose name was Ann Braswell. He contacted her and set up a revival meeting. God was really blessing and many souls were being saved. Ken and Debbie had been married about 10 years at this time. They came down to attend the revival. After the sermon one night, they went forward to the altar for prayer. Evangelist Ann prayed for Ken and Debbie and another couple named Bill and Barbara Copley. She told both couples that God was going to bless them and give them the desires of their heart. We were bouncing off the walls thinking that Debbie would become pregnant soon. She and Ken had spent a ton of money on every procedure possible and they still didn't have a baby. We knew that both couples desperately wanted children. Ken and Debbie went back home and we waited for news. Within two months we got the word that Bill and Barbara were expecting. I was happy for them and we waited for the news from our kids. As the months passed, I got discouraged, and then my discouragement turned to bitterness. I could not understand why we weren't getting a baby too. The Bible says that God winks at ignorance. During that time I know he winked a lot, because I was ignorant enough too gripe at Him. I told Him that He wasn't being fair. I am so glad that God is a God of love and compassion. He overlooked my ignorance and would prove that He had things under control all the time.

Lisa, Jack and their boys had been living in Brookport for a few years and by now they had moved back to DeKalb. Jack had gotten a job working for the 3M Company. Lisa had not been feeling well and got the news that another little one was on the way. Ryan and Kyle were 9 and 7 years old and like it had been with us, diapers in the house were a thing of the past! Jerry happened to be in the hospital having a surgery when Lisa went into labor. She had been in touch with us and said they would call whenever the baby was born. Well, as when Kyle was born, she called us herself and gave us the news. It was another boy, making 5 grandsons for us. His name was Tyler Allen, giving them a Ry, Ky and now a Ty, with a second name after Uncle Kenneth Allen.

The surgery Jerry had when Tyler was born didn't go well and he just couldn't seem to get back on his feet. Being discouraged, in September of 1994 we left Brookport as pastor and moved to Rochelle for a time of sabbatical from the ministry.

Jerry and I both got jobs and we bought a house. It was nice to live near Lisa's family and watch Tyler grow. We had been there just over a year when Don and Marilyn told us the Church of God in Cherry Valley, Arkansas needed a pastor. If we moved there, I would be near Mom. Several years after Dad's death, she had remarried, to a good man named Cecil Williams. He thought of us as his kids. After a unanimous vote, we moved to Cherry Valley in November of 1995. Mom had back surgery while we lived there and I was able to help with her care. We also saw Don and Marilyn pretty often, even though they were living in Pine Bluff. When Jerry needed a break or we were just plain bored, we'd call them or they would be calling us and we would get together for the night. The move was not the best thing for us, health wise and church wise, and after a year, we decided to move back to Brookport again, this time to retire.

Jack loved Brookport and the slow pace of living and after only two years up north, he had convinced Lisa a few months earlier to move back. Again, Jerry and I both worked and we finally settled in and we were happy. Jerry and Jack had a job working nights for a pharmaceutical company and I worked days for the same attorney Lisa was working for. The guys would take turns driving to work. Jerry had a cute little black truck and Tyler loved Grandpa and his truck. Every time Jerry would go to pick up Jack, Tyler would come running out and get in the truck.

Lisa and Jack bought Tyler a little black truck he could ride in and peddle. He thought it looked just like Paw Paw's. He and his Paw were big buddies. He never liked me very much and I was always trying to win him over. His third birthday was coming up. I told him I'd pick him up and we'd go to WalMart and he could pick out a birthday gift, then we'd go to the Dairy Queen for supper and he could play on the playground. He wasn't to sure he wanted to go, but finally gave in. (Lisa bribed him with money…..How sad!) We got our shopping done and headed for the car. I asked him if he was ready for the Dairy Queen playground and he said "no". I asked, "Don't you want to get something to eat and play for a while"? Again, he said "no!" I asked "what *do* you want to do." He replied, "I want to go to my house."

I responded "okay, we'll go to your house." He said to me, "No, *I* want to go to *my* house and I want *you* to go to *your* house!" In his three year old way, he was telling Grandma to **go home**!

I tried and tried to get him to like me, but to no avail! Finally, I started name calling…….I was a **bad Grandma**! Whenever I saw him, I called him horse breath or dog face and guess what? He would laugh and laugh. Soon we became friends but I have never let him forget the 3rd birthday shopping trip. At this writing, he has his driver's license and has a black truck. Best of all, we are good buddies.

I was still working for the Attorney and one day I got a call from a friend who asked if Ken and Debbie would be interested in adopting a baby. I told her maybe so…..why? She told me about a woman near Carbondale, IL, who was about to give birth and was planning to give the baby away. The woman was a dwarf and unmarried. There would be no way she could take care of a baby. I called Ken and told him about the baby and asked him to talk it over with Debbie. I said "there is one catch, the Mother is a dwarf. There is a strong possibility the baby might be dwarfed too." He said he'd call me back. In an hour or so, he called and said "Mom, we want the baby no matter how it comes out. We just want a baby to love and care for." The plan was in the works and the right parties were notified. In a couple of weeks I got a call at work that the birth Mother was possibly going into labor. The Doctors didn't want her to have a normal delivery due to her size. They had planned for her to have a C-section. I called Ken and they quickly packed a bag and were on their way to Carbondale.

From my Heart and Soul

On February 12, 1998, I headed for the hospital after work and got there right after this little bundle of 3 pounds, 5 ounces was delivered. We had a 50/50 chance of finally getting a granddaughter. I'm sure God smiled and maybe winked as they told me the baby was a boy! Didn't matter, he was beautiful. Even though he was very small, he seemed to be doing well. Ken and Debbie named him Samuel Evans Holt. They took Samuel from the Bible, and Evans after Debbie's Dad. Sam was born in a college town and several people wanted interviews and had questions concerning the birth Mother's dwarfism. Several Doctors took tests and discovered that the gene that causes dwarfism was not found in the baby.

For that we were thankful. Debbie stayed with us so she could be close to the baby and Ken had to get back to work. Leaving was a hard thing for him to do. After all these years of waiting for a baby, I guess he was afraid it would turn out to be a dream. It wasn't a dream….well, maybe a dream come true. We chose to call it a miracle. Debbie would give us an update every night. I will always remember the day Sam's weight reached 4 ½ pounds and he could be leave the hospital. Ken took another week off work and came back down to take his boy home. They brought him to our house and spent the night, before returning to their home in Aurora, IL. It was a joy, I'll never forget.

Chapter Seventeen

The Third Man

Jerry continued to work at the Pharmaceutical Company. One night in August, 1997, he came in early and his skin looked gray and pale. He said he was having bad chest pains. I rushed him to the hospital (he wouldn't let me call an ambulance) and sure enough he *was* having a heart attack. The next few months would prove to be a testing of Jerry's health. He had had several heart catheterizations done and had several Coronary Stents put in. The Doctor officially "retired" Jerry at this point. In 2000 he had to have open heart surgery to bypass four arteries. The surgeon called the children and I into a conference room and told us things went well, but he figured Jerry might only have another five years. I didn't want Jerry to know this; afraid he would just give up. He mended surprisingly well. He was able to fill in for ministers in the area and seemed to be doing well physically.

In October of 2003, a church where Jerry had filled in, contacted him to be their pastor. We prayed about it for several days and felt it was the right thing to do. We moved into the parsonage of the High Point Pentecostal Church and enjoyed a much larger house there. We just closed up our home in Brookport. After just a few months, Jerry started having problems again with his heart. His Doctor sent him to Vanderbilt

Hospital in Nashville, TN to see a heart specialist there. Lisa went with us for the first Dr's appointment. Jeremy came up from Cleveland. Jerry wound up having another heart catheterization. Lisa, Jeremy and I stayed in a hotel there and were able to take him home the next day. Just a couple of months later his condition had worsened. He could not walk out to the mail box without having a lot of pain. It was then we were told that nothing more could be done. It is quite a sobering feeling to be told you have a life threatening condition and nothing medically could be done to help. Jerry continued to pastor and we prayed.

One day a surgeon at Vanderbilt called Jerry personally, and told him that he had studied the catheterization video tapes and he felt he might be able to help. A new stent was on the market and it was being used successfully. Arrangements were made and soon we were on our way back down to Nashville. The surgeon was formerly from a leading hospital in Boston. He talked to Jerry, Lisa and me, about the procedure. Jerry had one artery that had been bypassed during the open heart surgery and that artery had three stents in it. The Doctor wanted to open that artery up. He said it was an artery, if working properly, would give Jerry a lot more blood flow. He said there was a chance of 0-5 percent of the procedure being successful. It was a long shot, but worth the effort. The doctor would insert a wire, but not force it, for fear he would puncture the artery and Jerry could bleed to death before they got his chest opened up to mend it. It was scary, but we felt it was the only chance we had. They wanted to save Jerry's surgery until the end of the day, so they could take the extra time they might need. It was finally done very late in the day and the Doctor came out smiling, telling us it was successful and not nearly as difficult as he had anticipated. Jerry didn't get put in a hospital room until nearly midnight. Lisa and I went to a hotel nearby and returned the next morning. Jerry told us an amazing story.

He said during the surgery (they kept him awake for it) he saw another man in surgical garb, enter the operating room and stand to look over the surgeon's shoulder. Jerry said when that man looked at him, Jerry noticed how his eyes were penetrating and full of love and kindness. At that precise time the surgeon was able to put the wire all the way through the three stents in that artery. The man looked at Jerry again, with smiling eyes, and then walked out. That morning Jerry asked the surgeon who the third man was and the surgeon said "no one was in there except the nurses and my assistant, we don't allow anyone to just walk in during surgery." Well, I truly believe it was the Lord or an angel of the Lord who went in to make sure the work was done correctly. Even after all this, I guess I was afraid and encouraged him to stop the pastoral work. The church understood and we moved back into our house at Brookport. The strength he gained was amazing.

Chapter Eighteen

Our Family Increases

Ryan had been seeing a cute girl named Emily Rust. She was a blond and beautiful. He had given her an engagement ring and they had set the date for July 31, 2004. When they heard we were selling our old house, Ryan approached us about selling it to them. With the house being old, Jerry really didn't want to sell it to them, knowing Ryan wouldn't know how to fix anything that might go wrong. Both kids insisted and we gave in. We sold it to them and moved. Emily's mother and Grandmother came over and repainted everything. It looked like a doll house when it was ready for them to move in. Time came for the wedding and it was a beautiful day and a beautiful wedding.

From my Heart and Soul

Kyle had been seeing a girl named Megan Brandon and things had been serious for a long time, even though he was still in school. She was a petite thing with beautiful dark eyes and hair. Megan was the granddaughter of a man who had served as the Treasurer of our church in Aurora many years prior. During the summertime, Megan's mother, Becky, had been a regular fixture in our home when she and Lisa were young. Becky's mother had passed away when she was five or six and Becky was being raised by her sister in southern Illinois. She spent a part of the summer in Aurora and stayed with us a lot. At that time we would have never guessed that their lives would be intertwined by Lisa's son marrying Becky's daughter. Kyle bought the ring and they set the date for July 1, 2005. In less than a year Lisa and Jack were gaining 2 daughters. Kyle and Megan bought a nice little house in Vienna, Illinois. Of course it needed painting, so the family pitched in and got things ready. The date came for the wedding and it was beautiful. After a honeymoon to the Dominican Republic, they settled in Vienna. At this writing, both couples have since bought larger, nicer homes. Ryan and Emily live in Paducah, Kentucky and Kyle and Megan live in the country near Dixon Springs, Illinois.

A few years prior, Lisa, Sherle, Debbie and I decided to do a Christmas ornament exchange during the Thanksgiving holiday. We would go shopping the day after Thanksgiving, then stop to eat lunch and have the exchange during the meal. Each one of us would try to find the most unique ornament and buy one for each woman. I will say that I gained a lot of beautiful Christmas ornaments in those few years. Of course the girlfriends wanted to get in on the exchange. I said "No!" I wanted this to be reserved for the married females in the family. Emily was so happy when she married first and got to be a part of the exchange that following Thanksgiving. Megan waited patiently and her turn came the following year. The six of us have had a lot of fun with this tradition.

In June of 2008, Emily gave birth to a beautiful little girl and they named her Rylee Peyton. She captured our heart. I never thought much about being a great grandmother, but soon found it to be wonderful. Although Rylee is a Daddy's, Popee's and Paw Paw's girl, I love her dearly. I heard her call me MawMaw for the first time a few days ago. It made me laugh. Watching her grow brings back a lot of memories of raising Lisa. At the moment, Rylee is not quite as domineering as her "Meme" was. Of course she doesn't have a brother or sister yet, to boss around. It's been a long time since Jerry and I have had a little one around the house. Her visits bring joy and laughter to us.

Everyone loves a baby whether they are related to it or not. A little one brings smiles, joy and warmth to our heart. I have wondered if that's how God feels when we are birthed into His family. Most children want to do things their own way. We say "don't touch, that's hot" and they touch, or "don't throw the ball inside the house, you'll break something," and they do." I guess we learn from experiences. Rylee may do her own thing and wind up getting a "booboo." Ryan and Emily will kiss it to make it better. We, as adults are just like children. Whenever we fall and our "heart" is skinned up, God is there to pick us up and brush us off. There are times when Rylee is exhausted from playing and won't settle down to nap. Her Mommy and Daddy know she needs to rest. They will caress her and gently stroke her hair and she falls asleep in their arms. Whenever you are heart broken and wounded, have you ever felt God stroke your hair?

Chapter Nineteen

The Vacation That Was Not to Be

In early 2006, I took a leave of absence from my job at the Law Office and went to work for the City of Brookport. The Village clerk had surgery and they needed someone to fill in temporarily for her and as a favor to the Mayor, I consented.

The job became quite involved when the Treasurer resigned. I was asked to stay on and take that position as a board appointed person. After careful consideration, I called my boss at the Law Office and gave him my resignation. The village board let me go ahead and keep my scheduled vacation in May. I guess the most difficult time in my life came at this point. We were to attend a Holt family reunion, the High School graduation of Nicholas and Jerry was to preach a weekend while we were gone. I had all the packing done so we could leave on Friday before Memorial Day. I told Jerry that I would only work a half day and come home so we could leave around 2 pm. I had laughingly, laid down the orders for him to be showered and dressed when I got home. While he loaded the car, I could vacuum the house and we would be ready to leave. When I got home just after 12:30, I smiled when I saw his truck in the driveway. I went into the house and didn't see him and just figured he was still showering. As I entered the bedroom, I didn't see a light on in the bathroom and I didn't find him there.

A year or so before, he had talked me into letting him buy a small Honda 250 Rebel motorcycle. He really enjoyed riding it and always wore a helmet. I knew he must be on that bike since he wasn't at home, so I started loading the car. I had made two trips to the car. As I was coming back in, the phone was ringing. I thought to myself, "yeah ole boy, you have ridden a little too far and you're running a little bit late......you are in big trouble!" I answered the phone and it was a girl who worked at the Law Office. She said, "Betty has Lourdes Hospital called you? Jerry has been in an accident." I just hung up on her and immediately called the hospital and reached the Emergency Room. They connected me with a nurse and she told me the news. He had been in a serious accident and had severe facial wounds with head trauma. She said to come quickly because he was being air lifted to Vanderbilt Hospital in Nashville.

I grabbed my purse and drove 85 miles per hour on Interstate 24, trying to get there as soon as possible. I had hoped a policeman would pull me over and give me an escort. That didn't happen. When I found Jerry in the ER, I was not prepared for what I saw. I had never seen that much blood. Most of his clothes had been cut off. His head was wrapped in gauze and blood was everywhere. He was tied to a gurney and screaming for them to untie him. I went to him and said, "honey, it's me, Betty." He screamed out, "oh, Betty untie me, please untie me, somebody untie me."

I tried to tell him that he had a motorcycle accident and was hurt pretty bad, but he just kept screaming out. As I tried to calm him, he let out a curse word. I gasped and looked at the nurse as I said "where did that come from?" The nurse said, Mrs. Holt, don't pay any attention to what he says. He has a head injury and there is no telling what he might say. He doesn't realize what is going on." Lisa came in about that time and her face drained of all its color when she saw the blood. I had her sit down and all she could do was cry. About that time the helicopter came and the medics started preparing

Jerry for the flight. We told him how much we loved him but I don't think he understood. He just kept screaming and struggling against the restraints on his wrists. They tried to assure us that he would be in good hands. We walked with them as they wheeled him to the helicopter.

We were asked to get in our vehicles, but, wait for the chopper to take off. As we waited, Lisa and I tried to make plans. She had rented a van at noon, because they were leaving on a vacation to Gatlinburg, TN very early the next morning. As we talked and waited, I saw Ada Copley, the Brookport Mayor and her sister, Wilma Burrus. About that time the chopper took off and we flashed our headlights and got their attention. Wilma and Ada insisted on driving me to Nashville so Lisa could go home and make plans for her family and join me as soon as possible. Wilma was driving 80 miles per hour, but it seemed to drag on forever.

We finally reached the hospital and found out where the trauma floor was. We walked in and I asked where they had put my husband. The nurse asked us to wait and soon a Doctor introduced himself to me and asked if we could go into a nearby room to talk. I began to tremble and cry. I said "just tell me, is he alive or dead?" The Doctor said "he's alive, but just barely. He explained that Jerry was in very critical condition with several broken bones and a severe brain trauma. A blood clot was forming.

He said "we are doing everything we can, but it just isn't enough." He asked me if I had children. I said "yes." He said "you need to get them here as soon as possible." They didn't think he would survive the night. The whole ordeal seemed to be a blur. How could this be happening?

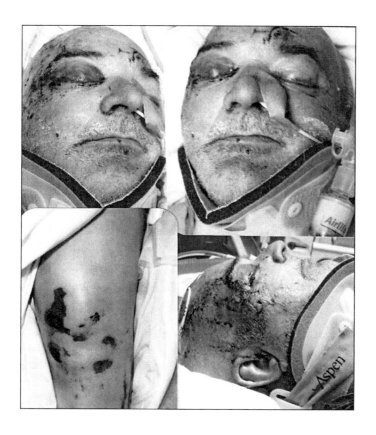

Pam Burden, a close family friend, had driven Lisa and they joined me shortly and Jeremy arrived. Ken and Debbie caught a plane and got to the hospital later in the evening. Jeff called to say he could not make connections to get a flight to Nashville until 5:30 the next morning. He was so upset. We both cried while talking on the phone. I told him that if something happened and his Dad didn't make it, I would call him immediately. Sherle said he didn't sleep all night. I was *there* with Jerry and I was in anguish so I understood how he must have felt, being so far away. All they could do was pray. Jerry's brother, Henry Jr., his wife Cindy and two of Jerry's sisters, Priscilla and Peggy got there from northern Illinois. A friend of ours, Vern Giltner, brought Jack and the kids to Nashville. Pastors, Charles Tate and Gaylen Stewart arrived. By midnight there were at least 20 people waiting and keeping a vigil. Lots of tears were being shed. If the nurse had not taken me to Jerry, I probably would not have recognized him. He looked much worse than he did back in the ER at Paducah. His head was swollen large and his face was cut and scraped up really bad. He was bleeding constantly because of the Plavix he had been taking due to his heart condition. That medication is not reversible, so they were giving him platelets and just let him bleed until the Plavix wore off. He had two skull fractures, a broken femur at the hip socket and broken neck bones. He had a broken kneecap, big toe and his little finger was almost severed at the first joint. The bones in the right side of his face were broken. Later we found out that the optic nerve to his right eye was damaged causing blindness in that eye. I stood there looking at the body of a man who had been my love for nearly 50 years and wondered if he would live. I had never seen him in this condition before. Lots of prayers were being said for him and I knew God was in control, but I will admit, I was scared to death.

I began to think of the times Jerry had cheated death. I wondered if his time might be up. I asked God to spare his life and not take him from me. I wanted him under any circumstance. Jeff was able to get to the hospital by mid morning. He had a hard time looking at his Dad. The feeling of helplessness was overwhelming.

After a couple of days people began to leave and go back to their homes. The kids and I discussed how they would take turns staying in Nashville with me. Day after day I stood beside Jerry's bed and wanted him to wake up. Each day there was no change.

They had operated on his leg to set it and put a rod in his broken femur. There was a hole drilled in his skull to let the fluid drain. A huge blood clot had formed and was pressing the brain to a very dangerous point. The technology there was amazing as they did everything they could to save his life.

Chapter Twenty

Three weeks of Trauma

I kept a journal of the next three weeks. Jeremy bought me a journal book and I filled in the first couple of days from memory, and then recorded each day. Even though it is written in bits and pieces, I have shared it here with you. It is from the actual journal.

Friday, May 26, 2006, Day 1

When we got to Vanderbilt, we went to the 10th floor…the Trauma Unit. A doctor Miller came out and told me Jerry had suffered severe brain trauma. He said "call your children home." They didn't think he would make it through the night. He had slipped into a coma. I can't express the despair and pain I felt. My heart broke. I was afraid I had lost him. Several people came to check on him. Friends from Brookport were there and we kept a vigil through the night. I can't explain how terrible he looked. We all prayed.

Saturday, May 27, 2006 Day 2

He has made it through the night. Still critical, touch and go. He has a blood clot on the right side of his brain about the size of a baseball, 2 skull fractures, a broken little finger, broken femur near the hip socket, broken neck bones, face bones and many cuts and scrapes and the right side of his head looks like ground beef, swollen and still bleeding. His right eyeball is a solid mass of red and still swelling. He is still alive and word has begun to leak out all over the country and people are praying. All the kids are here with me and we wait and pray. I have been at his bedside through many heart surgeries and heart procedures, but this is the worst I have ever seen him. All I can do is trust God. I feel so helpless. No words can describe how I feel.

Sunday May 28, 2006, Day 3

I sat up all night again. They wouldn't let anyone in the Trauma Unit so I waited. I maybe had gotten 2 hours of sleep in a waiting room chair when daylight came.

I figured the Doctors would make early rounds, but by 11:00 am, no word, nothing.

Ken just barged in the closed doors and asked "what's going on with my Dad?" He found out that Jerry had been moved to the third floor around 5:30 this morning and no one told us. It was a nightmare of anger and terror...everything! Jerry had been stable enough to move, yet still very critical and comatose. The situation on the third floor is better, less crowded, etc. I convinced Lisa and her family to go ahead with their plans for vacation. I told Jeff to go on back home. Nicholas would be graduating High School on Friday and it was Nick's week so make it special for him. I went to the motel and took Jeff's bed. Ken, Deb and Jeremy are still here.

Monday May 29, 2006 Memorial Day, Day 4

The day has brought little change in Jerry's condition. It is so hard to just stand by and know there is nothing I can do. I have kept him and taken care of him for 47 years and now have to stand back and let four teams of Doctors take over. Through all the prayers from all over the country, I know God is in control. Yes, I have asked Him WHY! In my heart I felt if He had planned to take him, Jerry would have died in the crash. God must not be done with him. Jerry continues to hang on. Debbie had to fly back home so Ken and I shared the motel room. Jeremy has gone home for a day or two to take care of some college business. He is to start back to college in summer classes for his Master's degree. I know that would make Jerry happy if he knew, but he is still comatose. Jerry had surgery on the broken femur today and it went well. A rod was put in his leg.

Tuesday, May 30, 2006, Day 5

Most everyone has gone home or on their trips. Ken is staying here with me. I know Jeff felt bad for leaving and Lisa too, but Jerry would want them to continue on with their plans. Ken helped me through some difficult moments today. I have always known that my kids were special, but in these times of trials, tests and trauma, they have proved their love for me and their Dad. Good kids are hard to find, but mine proved to be great! Brother Galen Stewart, Brother Charles Tate and Brother George Odell came today and brought love offerings. The Powerhouse church sent me a large goodie basket. God is already proving to me that He is in control. I have prayed and prayed…Jerry is still comatose.

Wednesday May 31, 2006, Day 6

When Ken and I got to the third floor, Charles Pugh, Buddy Chambers and Pastor Doug Stevens, all from the High Point Church in West Paducah, KY, were already there. They visited with us and prayed at Jerry's bedside. Brother Doug said he was going to call the hotel and pay for my room through June 6th. It was such a blessing. God has blessed us with financial blessings this week. I don't always understand how things or why things happen as they do, but I still trust God. It's hard to see Jerry with not much of a change in his condition. Jeremy came back today. He will stay with Ken and I till the weekend.

He got me a new cell phone. Jerry is still in a coma. Lord please let him know we are here with him.

Thursday, June 1, 2006, Day 7

Not a lot has changed. Ken has continued to send out emails to family and friends. Ken, Jeremy and I take turns staying in with Jerry. We have prayed together several times at his bedside and alone too. I have taken a cold with a sinus infection. I am plugged up. I make sure I sanitize my hands often. Bob and Linda will be here by Saturday morning. Ken will fly back home soon and Jeremy needs to get home too. It has been a tiring few days, but the Lord has kept us. I don't know where my strength has come from, except through God. I thank Him each day for Jerry being alive. Maybe soon he will wake up!

Friday, June 2, 2006, Day 8

This was a difficult day. The time had come for them to do a tracheotomy and put a screen in an artery to catch a clot, by chance one might develop. The tracheotomy was done in his room around 10:00 am. When we got to see Jerry it was a relief to see the ventilator tube out of his mouth. However, he started having a hard time almost immediately. He coughed and coughed through the tracheotomy tube. We noticed he yawned a couple of times and Ken saw that he had "tongued" the feeding tube (that had been down his nostril) up into his mouth. Ken told the nurse and she didn't believe him. When she checked Jerry, sure enough there it was and the Doctor told her to pull it out immediately and they would put another one back in later. We insisted they do the stomach feeding tube that afternoon when they put the screen in the artery. It finally got done and Jerry got to rest. Ken and Jeremy were going home and Ken came in to say good bye. My heart ached for him as he cried and prayed for his Dad. Jeremy had been his usual quiet self, but it was hard on him too, even though he would be back sooner then Ken. At the hotel we said our goodbyes and they left. I couldn't help but cry. Jerry is still in a coma.

An insert:
Jeremy had dropped out of college because a company had offered him a job making good money. He always promised his Dad that he would eventually go back to school and get his degree. He had finished up his classes and the first week of May in 2006, Jerry, Lisa, Jack and I went to Lee University in Cleveland, Tennessee, for his graduation. It was a wonderful day and we were happy for him. He decided to enroll during the summer months to study for his Master's degree. In looking back, I am so glad that Jerry had the opportunity to see Jeremy walk down the aisle to get his diploma that day. God was good to us

Saturday, June 3, 2006, Day 9
I awoke today thinking about the past week. God has brought us through a really rough time! His hand had spared Jerry during the accident and has kept him up till now. I've thanked Him every day! I called the Wilsons (the man who hit Jerry in the accident) and gave him an update on Jerry's condition. I asked him about the details of the accident. He said Jerry's helmet broke the glass on the driver's side window and his head hit the door post and bent it. Jerry was then hurled through the air and landed a few feet away. Mr. Wilson said he tried to help Jerry, and covered him with a jacket. He said Jerry fought against those who stopped to help. They actually held him down until the medics could get there.

Bob and Linda came today from Rockford. Jerry looked a lot better, but Bob had a hard time staying in there seeing his brother. Tonight Jerry's color looked better. He had been shaven (at my request) and he opened his eyes just a little when I called his name. I wonder if he will wake up tomorrow. I wonder if he has thoughts. I wonder how much longer we will be here. I wonder why, why, why!

Sunday, June 4, 2006, Day 10

It does not seem like Sunday. My days have all run together. Linda and Bob and I had our breakfast at the Hotel and headed for the hospital. Jerry was about the same visually, they said there were no signs of Pneumonia in the x-rays or culture tests! Praise God! Also they took him off the ventilator and he was breathing by himself through the tracheotomy tube. Vern and Hazel arrived by mid afternoon and stayed until the visiting hours were over at 5:00 pm.

My niece, Risa, who lives in the area, also came by. We all went to eat at Shoney's (except Risa.) She said she'd come by again tomorrow after work. Hazel brought a basket filled with goodies and also a card from Denny and Helen Kaylor with cash in it. A minister had come by from a Nashville church the other day. Today I had a message from a childhood friend of Jerry's, named, Tommy Duncan. The minister was Tom's Pastor and he heard about Jerry when the Pastor made a prayer request at the church. Tommy said he'd visit tomorrow. Jerry is still asleep. Lord, please let him wake up soon.

Monday, June 5, 2006, Day 11

Bob and Linda left this morning about 8:30 am. They offered to come back in a few weeks if I needed them. I went to the hospital for the 10:00 am visit. They took Jerry to surgery on his neck at 11:30. I went over to the hospital library and sent Ken an email, then went back to the second floor waiting room. I was given a sack lunch by a Church of Christ here in town. It tasted pretty good. The State Farm adjuster called me and said the bike was totaled and they would get the paper work started to pay us. Jeff came in around 3:30 pm. Jerry got back to his room around 5 p.m. We got to see him for a few minutes. We went to the hotel room, had some supper and then came back.

Tom Duncan came by to see Jerry. It had been 10 years since we had seen him. Jerry will have another surgery on his face tomorrow. I wonder when he will wake up. I'm getting anxious. His face was swollen today. I want to take him home...all well!

Tuesday, June 6, 2006, Day 12

Jeff and I came back to the hospital room. They were taking Jerry for surgery on his facial bones. We were told the surgery would take three hours. It would take an hour to transport him and get him prepared. We were called sooner. The surgery was successful and Jerry did well. The Doctor went in under his upper lip and his right lower eyelid. They pulled the depressed bones up and put in at least 3 plates. No external incision. Unbelievable!!! Tom Duncan came back with some people from his church. Their last name was Stoneburner. Tom offered his home to me and any family members who wanted to stay with me. I declined politely. They asked Jeff and I to come to their Wednesday night Bible Study and Supper Meal. We got directions and said we could be there. We have 3 ½ hours between day and evening visiting hours. We need to leave the Hotel room tomorrow and find another place to stay. Nashville Fan Fest is coming to town and the Hotel has been booked for weeks in advance. We have reserved another room 12 miles out. Jerry's face was very swollen but he seemed to be resting when we left at 10:00 pm.

Wednesday, June 7, 2006, Day 13

Jeff and I checked out of the Hotel and came back to visit Jerry. He was still swollen and still in a coma. The Duncans called me again offering their home to us. After talking to the kids, they thought I should accept. I called Tom and accepted his offer. He gave Jeff directions to their home and church. We stayed with Jerry all day and had to leave around 5:00 pm. We went to the Duncan's home first. It's huge and very beautiful!

Betty Duncan is such a caring person. We went on to church and had dinner and enjoyed a very informal Bible Study. We left at 8:00 pm to go back and see Jerry. He looked better, but still in a coma. We stayed until visiting time was over and headed back to the house. I have access to 3 bedrooms each with a private bathroom. The Duncans want to make sure I have everything I need. I know I will rest well and thank God for taking care of me and Jerry. I am still praying for him to wake up and recognize me.

Thursday, June 8, 2006, Day 14

Jeff needed to go home and help Nick pack for his move to Georgia. He decided to fly and leave his car here in Brentwood at the Duncans, (since he will be coming back through after moving Nick to Savannah.) I dropped him off at the airport and went on to the hospital. Lisa is coming tomorrow. The Duncans are glad for us to be here to house sit for them…they are taking a trip to Rockford, Illinois. Jim and Gwen Jones came by on their way to see Pam (their daughter.) They both cried at Jerry's bedside. We had prayer and we visited for about 30 minutes in a waiting room before they left. I have had many people stop by from the Nashville area. Keith Manley was here with Jimmy Snow's wife. Jerry got a card from the recording studio where Keith records. Bishop Don and Sissy Stovall came by 2 times. Our State and National Headquarters for the Church of God sent $500 each. Bishop Stovall said an offering was taken at Camp Meeting and it was $1300.00. He will mail it to me. Pam Burden had been kind enough to loan me a Sprint cell phone. There is a Sprint tower within the hospital. My Verizon does not get out well inside the building. I've had so many calls asking about Jerry and offering assistance and prayers. God has some good and caring people. Jerry is still recovering slowly. Still in a coma.

Friday, June 9, 2006, Day 15

I came in this morning to see Jerry and he seemed to be responding better. He has moved his left arm twice just a little. He moves his right hand a lot. I've seen him turn his head just a bit even though he's in a neck brace. I stayed in town all day today. Anthony and Dee De Tinnin and their children came by to see Jerry. They offered to take me to dinner, but I had eaten a late lunch and wasn't hungry. I needed to go to Walgreen's to get some things and they went along. Anthony gave me a gift card for $20 and another $30 in cash. I went back to the hospital and sat in the waiting room and visited with a lady whose husband is on the third floor also. Lisa and Pat Giltner got to the hospital at 10:00 pm. The nurses let them go back to see Jerry. We left the hospital around 10:30 pm and came back here to the Duncan's.

Saturday, June 10, 2006, Day 16

Lisa, Pat and I went to the Cracker Barrel for breakfast then on to see Jerry. He seemed to respond much better today. The Duncans called to check on Jerry. They are now in Wisconsin. Debbie Fernatt Bock came by to visit again and Lisa didn't recognize her. We had a good chat. We left the hospital around 5 pm and went to eat. The girls wanted to go to the Red Lobster. I had grilled shrimp. Went back to the hospital to see Jerry. Lisa and I were kidding around and really believe he was tickled inside. He raised his left eyebrow and had a slight grin on his face. I wonder what he is thinking. I wonder if he knows we are with him. He is improving slowly. The Doctors talk of sending him to a skilled nursing home to recover. He can't go home yet. Still not quite awake to respond. I am anxious to take him home.

Sunday, June 11, 2006, Day 17

Lisa, Pat and I went to see Jerry. He looked even better than yesterday. The girls left and went to a mall and bought me some "Crock" shoes. My feet are so tired. I have to stand most of the time in Jerry's room and I am exhausted. Pam got here this afternoon to stay with me and Lisa and Pat are going home. Jeff, Sherle, Nick and the Groovers (Sherle's parents) came by tonight to see Jerry. They are moving Nick to Savannah, GA to live with Brandon. Sherle and Nick cried. Jeff's church sent $600 to us and Jack Groover gave me $100. I got a card from Edgar and Andrea Foster and they sent $100. God is blessing us financially. I want Him to bless me with a whole husband. I'm standing on His promise and believe Jerry will be well.

Monday, June 12, 2006, Day 18

Today was the day I've waited for! Jerry had a lot of company and had sat in a special chair most all day. He didn't respond a lot today so the nurses put him back in bed with a patient lift. Pam and I went back to the hospital for the 8 pm visit. He heard my voice talking to the nurse and opened his eyes and was looking for me. Pam called "he is awake, come here." I stepped to his bedside and asked him for responses. On command, he wiggled fingers, waved his hand, squeezed my hand and reached up and tried to scratch his nose. He tried to put his hand on top of his head like he usually sleeps. I cried, Pam cried and it was really exciting! I told him some of what had happened to him and explained the neck brace and the tube in his windpipe. I told him he was getting better and God had touched him. I've not been back home since the accident happened, but I have high hopes of getting him home soon. Thank God for answered prayers. Praise His name!

Tuesday, June 13, 2006, Day 19

Pam and I went back to the hospital. Jerry was still responsive. He is getting better each day. I don't know just how much he really knows. We stayed all day then went back to the Duncan's house. Betty Duncan had some chicken and rice and insisted we eat. They have been really nice to us. Betty and

Tom had a meeting to attend and Pam and I headed back to see Jerry. After their meeting, Betty and Tom came by for a visit. Betty had not visited Jerry yet. I was told by the Stoneburners that Tom was taking this pretty hard. They said he talks about old times with Jerry quite a bit. The third floor is talking about moving Jerry upstairs tomorrow. I am looking forward to moving him home with me. I hope it is soon.

Wednesday, June 14, 2006, Day 20

Today, Lisa came. She got to the hospital before noon. The case worker named Jackie has been talking to me about placing Jerry in a Rehab Center. He was moved to the 11th floor today. It is an overflow of the ICU. I had a hard sell on sending Jerry to Calvert City, Kentucky, to a Nursing and Rehab Center. Every place I wanted him to go does not have a room for him. I finally gave in to the place in Calvert City. I don't have peace about it. Lisa, Pam and I stayed at the hospital all day until the 10 pm visit was over. I was upset at the Calvert City move. I want him closer to home than that. When we got back to the Duncan's house I cried. I feel so unsure of all this. I was told he may be moved tomorrow. I'm really tired. Tomorrow will be three weeks, here, away from home. Jerry didn't respond much today. I pray Lord, please guide this move. I don't know what I'm doing.

Thursday, June 15, 2006, Day 21

This morning my cell phone rang early. Our family Doctor's, nurse called to say relax, Jerry would be brought to Metropolis (just 10 miles from home.) He would go to the local hospital there before going to the Rehab facility. The Rehab does not have a bed available right now, but expect to have one soon. I felt it was an answer to prayer. The Doctor had to pull some strings, but Jerry would be close to home. Lisa and I went on to the hospital and Pam headed back to Brookport. We were told that Jerry would be moved by ambulance at 10 am the next day. And also, that Medicare would pay for it.

God has truly answered prayer. I can sleep well tonight knowing I'll be home tomorrow. I have had a very nice room and private bath in a beautiful house, but there is no place like home. Lisa and I stayed all day at the hospital. We went out to buy a gift for Betty, for all her hospitality. She has really been a blessing to me!

Friday, June 16, 2006, Day 22

I packed my suitcase and put clean sheets on the bed and cleaned my bathroom before going downstairs. Lisa and I said our goodbyes to the Duncans and headed for Vanderbilt hospital. We met Bobby and Tina Wiley in the hall. They had been to see Jerry and we had missed them. Their son is in the Children's Hospital here. The ambulance arrived at 10 am. A whole ream was preparing Jerry for transport. Near 11 am they took him downstairs and Lisa and I headed to our cars. We got to the Massac Community Hospital not long after the ambulance arrived. They already had Jerry in a bed. The room was quiet and there were chairs! I have had to stand for 3 weeks while visiting him. Lisa and I stayed for a couple of hours then left. I went home for the first time in three weeks. Things looked good, a little dusty, but I was glad to be home. I stayed a couple of hours and went back to see Jerry. Lisa rode with me. Jack and Tyler came by later. Jerry seemed to be resting. He had made us laugh. The nurses had put an oxygen cup over the tube in his neck, and he had pulled the cup up on his forehead. It looked so funny. I bent down to kiss him and he hugged me real tight!

I won't share the whole journal but we liked having Jerry in the hospital near home. He received excellent care there. The nurses were so gentle with him. For some reason, Jerry didn't want to keep a hospital gown on. We would find him completely naked lying there, his eyes open but he was in another world. He did not know us most of the time. Other times he made us laugh by the things he would do.

Ryan had figured the cupboards would be bare since I had been gone for three weeks. He brought a lot of groceries over. When I got home from seeing Jerry that evening, I was able to put them all away. Jeff and Sherle got to the house around midnight and we sat up until 1:30 am. I tried to catch them up on Jerry's condition. Ken would get in the next day. The boys with the help of Wayne Jenkins and Wayne's grandson and also Jack and Ryan would put a new roof on our house. They just about suffered heat exhaustion. They returned in a few weeks and built a ramp off the back deck so we would be able to get Jerry in the house. It was turning into a hot summer. Jerry was improving slowly, but got agitated easily. The tracheotomy tube kept him from speaking and it was difficult for him to make us understand. The nurses weighed him and he had lost over 40 pounds.

Ken stayed on after Jeff and Sherle went home. Before the accident, I had heard that Don Williams was coming to Paducah on a final concert tour. He was one of my favorite singers. Jerry liked him too. I had told Jerry I wanted tickets to the concert for my birthday present. Well I soon forgot about that with all that had happened. Ken told me one day that he had to go to Wal-Mart and would be back in a little while. When he got back, he pulled 2 tickets out of his pocket and handed them to me. He said "Mom, you don't have to go if you don't want to, but I think you need a break and this will be good for you." I hated to leave Jerry, but Lisa said she would stay with him, so Ken and I went to the concert. I cried during a couple of the songs. Jerry had sung them to me over the years. It was a very nice gesture on Ken's part and I appreciated it.

On the 34th day since the accident, I was told that a room had been made ready for Jerry at the Nursing and Rehab Center and he would be moved the next day. I was dreading it. Around

3:30 that afternoon an ambulance moved him across town. I looked around and felt like a dirty dog for putting him in that place. The bottom bed sheet literally had 15-20 iron on patches. He was not on the wing they had promised he would be on. I cried silently the rest of the afternoon and into the evening. Lisa came after work and stayed with us. She tried to get me to go home, but I just couldn't leave him. Finally around 8:30 pm, I was exhausted and headed for home. I sent the boys an email and said "I hope your Dad forgives me for this move." It had been a bad day and I cried myself to sleep that night.

The next day, I sent Lisa to WalMart to buy a nice mattress cover and two sets of sheets. The bedding looked a lot better, but it did not change the unsanitary conditions. I saw a nurse pour meds and water down his feeding tube without putting on gloves. I came in one day and they were cleaning his tracheotomy tube and didn't have on sterile gloves. His neck brace was off and no one was holding his head to keep him from moving it. I watched as they cleaned his soiled body and pile the soiled washcloths on the bedside table near his head. Needless to say, I reported this to the head nurse. Jerry did get moved to the right wing after I made a huge fuss. (After he came home I reported the Nursing and Rehab Facility to the state of Illinois. They got reprimanded.)

The 4th of July had arrived and I sat reading or doing a puzzle while Jerry slept. I heard a noise and looked up to find my cousin, Aggie Pavone and her daughter Michelle and grand daughter Samantha standing there. Aggie came all the way from Maine. She had visited Michelle in St. Louis and they surprised us with a visit. Jerry knew them and we had lots of hugs. I left the Rehab and went to lunch with them. That day I thought of my brother Dewey. This was his birthday. He would have been 73 years old if he had lived.

In just four more days, I spent my 63rd birthday sitting there at Jerry's side. It was a boring day. I guess I was feeling a little sorry for myself. Under normal conditions, Jerry would be taking me out to dinner at a nice restaurant. I knew there would not be a dinner tonight. That afternoon, Lisa and Jack brought me a bouquet of pink carnations, my favorite flower, and the card read, "All my love, Jer." I still have the card. I knew that Jerry had not bought the flowers, but Lisa didn't want me to go through my special day without a gift from her Dad.

One day I went to see him and found his tracheotomy tube had been removed and he could speak! I was so surprised and happy. Just to hear his voice even though it was weak and scratchy and to hear him call my name was such a treat! Eventually, he started having a lot of company and began telling things that he imagined were true. He told everyone he was a song writer, country music singer, government agent with nine firearms in his room and a collector of vintage cars. He kept everyone laughing. His voice had gotten much stronger. The nurses would ask him to sing one of the songs he had written and he would start singing. "Your Cheatin' Heart," or the "Tennessee Waltz." I don't know why he picked those two songs, but he was adamant that he had written them! He sang them proudly, but I must say, not in his best singing voice!

One day when a male nurse gave him his meds through the feeding tube, I asked "tell me what you just gave him. "He listed all the meds I knew Jerry was taking and added coumadin. I asked "why coumadin" and he replied, "Well, Mr. Holt has an order for it." Later, after investigating, I found, it had indeed ***not*** been ordered and Jerry was getting someone else's medication. The Administrator denied it, saying it was only recorded on Jerry's chart in error. I knew that was not the truth! Most of his care was bad and I started to make arrangements to bring him home. I ordered a hospital bed and all the things I would need to care for him. The Doctor and the Rehab Administrator were not happy with me, but I didn't care. Jerry needed sterile care and I knew I could give it to him better than what he was getting there.

Channel 6 in Paducah, KY got word of his accident and called to ask if we would give them an interview. I consented and Jerry and I sat and talked to the reporter for several minutes. We were on the 6 o'clock News that evening. I tried to emphasize the importance of wearing a helmet. Even though Jerry was wearing one, he still had an irreversible brain injury. After the interview, I told the reporter that he was coming home the following Saturday and she asked if they could come to the house to film it. Jerry had told me of a dream he had. He dreamed, when he went home, the yard was full of people welcoming him. When Ryan heard about the dream, he started the ball rolling and a gathering was in the works.

Chapter Twenty-one

Home at Last but Not For Long

Finally on August 5, 2006 Jerry came home with a police escort and a caravan of cars. Over 65 people were in our driveway waving hello to him. It was an exciting day! Channel Six was there to film his homecoming and again we were on the 6 o'clock news. Jerry's brother, Bob and his wife Linda, and also his sister, Peggy, came back down to help me bring him home. They have been faithful to check on Jerry. Bob and Linda came in June to Vanderbilt and here in July and again back in August. On Sunday morning they were all getting ready to go back home. Peggy had things to attend to at her work and would be back on the following Wednesday. Since Bob was retired, Jerry wanted him to stay. He seemed afraid for Bob to leave. Bob tried to explain that they needed to go back home so Linda could get back to work. Jerry smarted off, "let her go on home. You don't work, you can stay." Bob was near tears when they left. It was so hard for him to see Jerry like this. The brothers are only 11 ½ months apart in age and share a real closeness

Jerry's homecoming soon turned bad. He was home only four days and coping with him was quite a handful. His sister, Peggy, had just returned and was there to help me. That afternoon, Jerry started crying out in pain. We didn't know what the problem was and thinking it better to be safe rather than sorry, we called an ambulance. He was admitted to Western Baptist Hospital in Paducah, with some complications he received from lack of care in the Nursing and Rehab Facility. After a week, he was on the right track and the neurosurgeon thought a stay in a Specialized Rehab Facility in Paducah would help him. We checked him in and he went through 3 weeks on intense Physical and Occupational Therapy. He finally got home to stay. It was mid September. From May 26th to mid September, Jerry had been home only four days. I thought the ordeal was finally over. The truth was the real ordeal was only beginning!

The next few months would prove to be a very trying time for me being his caregiver. I didn't realize it, but, he was being overdosed by the Doctors. They had him on Abilify, Paxil, Seroquel, Requip, Clonazepam, Ambien CR, Trazodone and Zanax. Most of them were given at the same time. Evidently the two Doctors were not looking closely at his med list. I didn't know exactly what they all were for. With him being diabetic, his blood sugar stayed sky high, no matter what I fed him. The insulin just wouldn't keep it in check. He only slept 20-30 minutes at a time, even though some of the meds were for sleeping. The rest of his waking time, he was trying to climb the walls, or screaming and trying to get out of his bed. One night he screamed out to me twelve times in just an hour. He thought I had rented the house out to hospital personnel and didn't like it that "those people" had just taken over our house. He hallucinated about everything. The hospital bed had been set up in our den, so he could have access to the TV. At night, during his ravings, I would go in, time after time and beg him to calm down and sleep. This was "not" the husband I knew and I wanted my husband back!! I cried and prayed, wondering why God had forsaken us. I had about reached the end of my rope and was about to throw in the towel. I prayed to die and ask God to take my life and Jerry's too at the same time. I was living on about 3 hours of sleep a night and that was in cat naps. I was about to drop. After doing some internet research, of the meds he was on, I began to slowly take him off some of them without telling the Doctor. I began to see a slight improvement.

He finally reached a point where he could sleep in our King Sized bed with me. I had the Medical Equipment Company come and get the hospital bed. I would put a guard on his side of the bed so he wouldn't roll off. I was able to get a little more sleep. The nearness of me lying there beside him helped some. He still hallucinated. One night he woke me up and said, "Betty, a man just walked past the bed and went into our bathroom." He said "get up and check on it!" I was startled at first. Then, I realized the door locks were dead bolted and I was not a sound sleeper, so I didn't believe him. I refused to get up and check and he became furious with me. He wanted to fight and tried to strike me. This type of thing happened often. The neurosurgeon had warned me to keep my distance when he was like this, for fear he might actually hurt me. One night he told me to get up and check on something and I said things were okay and asked him to go to sleep. To my surprise, in the dark, he landed a blow to my face. It didn't hurt that much, but startled me. Since he had lost so much weight, I decided to physically subdue him. He had enough mentality to realize I was stronger than he was. That never happened again. He would still wake me from a sound sleep to say that someone was knocking on the door. I got up to check the first few times, and then learned to lay there and wait until I heard the knock. It always turned out to be him dreaming or hallucinating. My body was tired and wearing out from the lack of real rest. I felt that I was sinking into a deep hole. It seemed that God didn't love us anymore. I yelled at God and asked Him "why?" I wanted to know what we had done to cause Him to forsake us. Each day I would go through the motions of everyday existence. I lost the man I had loved for over 50 years. Oh, he was here in the house, but most of the time he was in another world. I felt all alone. I was angry and hurt. I wanted to die, but then I feared

I would and worried at what would happen to Jerry. I tried to face the world as though nothing was wrong, but inside I was completely wasted. I needed help!

One day I received a book from my "secret sister" at church. The title was "Humor for a Friend's Heart." It had a lot of funny and serious stories from different writers in it. I tried to read it and just could not get "into" it. I wasn't in the mood to read "funny stuff" and I was too depressed to read anything serious. One day I tried again and read a story entitled "Quack Quack" written by Karen Scalf Linamen and one paragraph really spoke to me. It said *"Lord, hang on to me. I know I should be hanging on to you, but I'm not. The truth is, I feel too wounded and broken and angry and rebellious and hurt right now to hang on to you. So if I'm going to get through this at all, it's got to be up to you. See me through this, Lord, hang on, please hang on to me and don't let go."*

There before my eyes was a paragraph written by another woman and it described just how I felt. Wounded, angry, hurt, broken, abandoned and at that time rebelling toward God. I cried as I read it over and over again. I made this my prayer that day and also for the next several weeks after that. I could not form words for any other prayer! I had to trust Him! Isn't God amazing! When I felt I was falling into a great abyss, there He was to hold on tight to me. From that day forward, things began to change. By then, Jerry was off all the meds that seemed to make him crazy. I saw him changing for the better and I knew God was healing his brain and mind. We settled into a daily routine and our love began to grow. Don't misunderstand, we still had many battles to conquer, but God brought back laughter into our lives. Although the road has been rough, I'm thankful the Lord is letting me walk it with that boy who stole my heart when I was just 10 years old. Jerry, you remain the love of my life!

Chapter Twenty-Two

A Series of Firsts

Today, July 8, 2008, has been a number of firsts for me. I turned 65 years old. The first time I have ever been that old. Today my new little great grand daughter came to my house for the first time. She is less than three weeks old. Today we took a five generation picture. Another first. I was able to spend my birthday with my 91 year old Mother, brother and sister-in-law. That's a first. It has made me realize how we go through life and let the little things pass by without recognition. Mom has Alzheimer disease and I wonder how much longer we will have her. Each time I see her, I wonder if it will be the last time I see her alive. Ninety-one years is a long time to live. She wondered whose house this was and sometimes just who we were. She got lost the first night and couldn't find her way back to bed after she used the restroom. I doubt if I ever see ninety one years old. I'm not sure I want to. But birthdays happen and will never go away as long as we continue to see another day. Mine today has been great.

 My Mom was always a very neat freak and would not even go to the grocery store unless she was dressed up, complete with good wig and make-up just right. She stayed youthful looking for years. I remember on her 73rd birthday, the family gave her a party and I was not able to attend. She was dating a man who was a little younger than she was and she didn't want anyone to mention her age. In fact in a humorous way she threatened us with bodily harm if we told her real age. For some reason, the boyfriend thought she was 65 years old. Wonder where he got that idea?

For the occasion I wrote a poem and sent it for someone to read at the party. It went like this.

My Mother
When I was just a little girl
I thought you were old.
I didn't know your exact age
I guess I'd never been told.
But I could tell by looking
That you'd been around awhile.
I wasn't dumb and after all
I was you're ….. Fifth child.
But through the years as I matured
Something strange came to be.
For when I really looked at you
It seemed you looked like me.
Where have all the years gone?
I thought as I smoothed my brow.
How does she do it? She stays so young.
I must find out somehow.
The last time that I saw you
You looked so youthful to me.
I'll bet none of my friends would ever guess
That today you are…….yessiree My Mother!

On the last line, they paused and Mom gasped. She knew that "73" rhymed with the word "me" and was afraid that's how the poem would end. Since her boyfriend was there, he would surely find out her real age. I guess I fooled her!

Chapter Twenty-three

Fifty Years of Loving You

On February 14, 2009, Jerry and I celebrated our 50th wedding anniversary. A couple was hired to decorate the fellowship hall of the High Point Pentecostal Church. It was beautiful. Lisa, Sherle and Debbie stood up with me. Bob Holt (the original best man), Jeremy and Jack stood up with Jerry. Ken and Jeff conducted the reaffirmation of our vows. Jeff had gotten with Jerry and helped him to get together words that were in his heart. I had written my vows several weeks before and had memorized them backwards and forwards. When the time came, I started blubbering and could not get it together. Ken had to read them line by line for me to repeat. I had no idea that the moment would be so emotional for me. We had friends and relatives from several states to come and help us celebrate. It was a day Jerry and I will never forget. Our vows went as follows;

Betty's Renewal Vows

Jerry, fifty years ago on this day, I stood with you at an altar to pledge my love and faithfulness. The road we've traveled has been long. Sometimes the road was smooth, other times it was rough. Back then we pledged our love for better or worse in sickness and in health. At times there was more worse than better and sometimes more sickness than health. Together we overcame the obstacles that were against us. You have given me a lifetime of wonderful memories. We have rejoiced at the birth of three sons and a daughter, the marriage of two sons and a daughter bringing Sherle, Debbie and Jack into our lives. We rejoiced at the birth of six grandsons, the marriage of two grandsons and last year the birth of our first great granddaughter, Rylee. You have laughed with me, cried with me, prayed with me, and always been here for me. The last three years have brought a new meaning to our love. We have been tried as gold in the refiner's fire, and together we made it! So today I reaffirm my vow to you of undying love and faithfulness forever.

Jerry's Renewal Vows

Bet, I can't believe, that 50 years have already passed since we first said "I do." During the lean years, when we had no food in the house, you stood by my side as God provided. During the difficult years of ministry, you continued to stand by my side as God provided. And now in my weakness, you still stand beside me, and God still provides for us.

I can't thank God enough that He gave you to me. Though we've never really known what many consider the richer things of life, I consider myself the richest man on earth because of you. As I told you the other day, when we first said till death do us part, we should have said forever. If I had my way, that is what I would want to do, stay with you forever. Therefore, today I proudly renew my vow to you, before all our family and friends.

Chapter Twenty-four

My Mother

Several months have passed since I wrote about Mom. She reached her 92nd birthday and had been near death for several weeks. At that time, our 50th Anniversary was nearing and we got the call from Don that Mom was in the hospital and had a blood clot in her left leg. They didn't see how she could survive. Lisa, Jerry and I immediately went down on a Wednesday. She didn't know who we were and talked out of her head most of the time. Jeremy, who was working in Memphis at that time, came over. Giles and Sherri were on their way to our house, from Arizona, and stopped off in Arkansas when they got the news about Mom. We all sat there with Don and his wife Pam, just hating a disease that takes ones mind away like Alzheimer does. Everyone left, to go and get some sleep and Pam stayed at the hospital with Mom. I volunteered, but Pam said Mom was used to her being nearby and it would be better, if we didn't change Mom's routine any more than was necessary.

The next morning we went back to see her. She was in her right mind and we sat all day and laughed and talked. She seemed to know us and we told old stories and funny things that had happened through the years. She rallied and everyone went back home and Giles and Sherri headed to our house for the anniversary celebration.

On Friday after our celebration we went to Arkansas again because Mom had taken another turn for the worse. She had been sent home from the hospital to die. I had never been in this position before. This was my Mother and it was hard to see her like this. Mom had always been so youthful and now time and disease had taken its toll on her body. I was thankful that she seemed to be in her right mind. One night, Pam asked if I would come and talk with Mom, because she was becoming agitated. I had thought Mom had gone to sleep. I went in and sat down next to her bed and began to talk. I asked her if I could pray, because I felt she was troubled about something. I believe she realized that death was near and I wondered in my mind just what a person feels or thinks at a time like that.

I told Mom that everything would be okay and ask her if she was afraid of anything. With tears streaming down her face, Mom said, "I don't want to face God with sin in my life." I tried to comfort her and tell her that God knew and understood and she could make things right while we prayed.

My Mother began to pour out her heart and pray sincerely for the first time in years. She cried out in the strongest voice she had, asking God to forgive her for all the sin in her life. I remembered the stories I had heard about the Pentecostal church services in "days of old," where the power of God would come over Mom. She would take the globes off the kerosene lamps that were lighting the church and hold them in her hands as sinners ran to the altar to ask God for forgiveness. I wondered how long it had been since she had given that any thought. I wanted her to remember the good things that were done in her life. After we prayed we hugged and hugged and cried and cried. I told Mom that she had just given me the best gift she could have ever given to me. I saw laying there, the Christian Mother, who along with Dad, raised us in a God fearing and loving home and had given us Godly teaching as young children.

It seemed after Dad passed away, something happened to Mom. She lost sight of all spiritual things. She was on the go all the time and kept very late hours. She was doing things that she and Dad had taught me were wrong. I can remember the first time I ever saw her light up a cigarette. She didn't think I was anywhere around. It broke my heart, as did the time I found whiskey in her laundry room closet, while looking for cleaning supplies. I never looked down on her for this, but always wished I could see the Mother I knew when I was a young woman. Some family members have tried to tell me that Mom never felt she was doing anything wrong. But, as we prayed there that night and I looked into her face with tears streaming down, I knew that the years of fast lane living had caught up with her. God, as always, was there, waiting for His turn again in her life. Romans chapter 14, verses 11-12 says "For it is written, as I live, saith the Lord, every knee shall bow to me, and every tongue shall confess to God. So then every one of us shall give account of himself to God." This makes me believe, we can tell ourselves anything we want to hear and eventually we believe it, but when the time has come for that appointment and death is knocking at the door, we want to make sure we are ready for that final destination.

Mom rallied again and we decided to go back home. This time when I told her goodbye, I felt peace and was ready to let her go. After we got back home, I was driving through Paducah, KY on my way to a store. Due to an ice storm a few weeks earlier that caused severe tree damage, there were dead limbs everywhere. I passed through a wooded area and there was a large dead limb totally broken off from the tree, just lying on the ground. At the top of the dead limb were some budding, flowering blooms. There was no traffic behind me and I came to a stop. The Lord was trying to tell me something. It was as if Mom's body was the branch and her spirit was the flowering blooms. The branch looked as dead as it could be, but the beautiful color showed a glimmer of life and hope. The disease had stripped her mind away and other medical problems took away her weight and made her face gaunt and hollow cheeked. Her body was the tree branch, but her inner spirit, (the blossoms,) was still clinging on and waiting to see the face of God. She continued to hang on for another few weeks. On a Sunday afternoon I called to talk. Her voice was weak and she rambled a lot. I asked if she knew who I was and she said "yes." After we talked a few minutes, I told her I loved her and she replied "I love you too, honey." The following Thursday, on April 2, 2009, God called her name and she was ready to go. It was a bittersweet event for me. I knew she was in a better place, but the thought of losing her was a bitter pill to swallow. There is a southern gospel song that I love, and a line goes like this. "Save a place for me at the table beside you and tell everyone that I am on my way." One day I plan to see both my parents, in a place where we will never be apart again.

Chapter Twenty five

My Heritage

I consider myself blessed to be born into a Christian home and raised by Godly parents. When parents give their children proper teaching, it will stay with them. Oh, I know most kids are like I was, forgetting and sometimes losing their way. KJV Proverbs 22:6 says, "Train up a child in the way he should go: and when he is old, he will not depart from it." One definition of the word *train* in Webster's dictionary is, "to guide the mental, moral, etc. development of." They trained me to be honest, decent, to work hard and to love the land and make my life count. They **showed** me how to love God. The older I got, the more I appreciated the teachings of my Mom and Dad. They were mere sojourners in this land. They made their way, left their mark and have gone on to be at rest with the Lord Himself. We, who are still striving for that land, must make our way and leave a mark for those who come after us. When my life is over, I want to be remembered as a woman who loved God and her family, and also, whose life counted for something.

I am so proud of my family. I have had people ask me, "What is your secret to having well behaved kids who grow up to serve the Lord in ministry?" All I can say is this, Jerry and I have been blessed. We tried to set a good example and train them as best we could, but God gets the glory for whatever they have become. Jeff and Ken are Ordained Bishops in the Church of God Organization and serving as Pastors, Jeff in Florida and Ken in Illinois. Jeremy went on to teach school in Cleveland, TN., and is involved in the Tres Dias Ministries in his local area. Lisa has blessed our local church with her musical talent in choir leadership. Four of our six grandsons are ministers. Brandon is a Music Minister in the Jacksonville, Florida area and Nicholas is a Children's Pastor near Memphis, TN. Ryan and Kyle serve as Youth Ministers and musicians in our local church. Tyler blesses our church with leading praise and worship in the youth services. We are still waiting to see what God has in store for Sam. My granddaughters-in-law, Emily and Megan and my great-granddaughter, Rylee, have all encouraged me and brightened my life. Jerry and I have been blessed with the mates our married children have chosen. Sherle, Debbie and Jack, I love you three as my own.

I am so glad the Lord answered the prayer of that little 10 year old girl. I thank Him for the gift of music He has put in my life. I am thankful that the "gift" was bestowed on my children and grandchildren. Besides musical talents, the Lord has blessed us with a delightful sense of humor. When we get together, we all have a good time.

Jerry and I owe so much to our children. Since his accident, they have taken of their time and been here, to do work on our house or car or help with Jerry. Lisa lives just down the street and she is here several times a week to see that we are okay and to brighten the day of her Dad. Jack has been so faithful to do most of the mowing in the summer and snow shoveling in the winter. Our grand children have all helped along the way, either by a visit or telephone call. We are proud of them all and we will be forever grateful!

The Lord has molded my life and my children have enhanced it. It was their love and support that gave me the strength and encouragement to overcome some of the difficult times I have written about in this book. I trust you have enjoyed these stories that came from "My Heart and Soul."

Chapter Twenty-six

Poetry

Over the years I have written poetry just for my own enjoyment. I want to share some of it with you, here.

Jerry

My knees buckled, I almost fell when
I saw you lying there.
Your brain was hurt, your body broken,
blood was everywhere.

I felt so helpless and all alone; there was nothing
I could do.
My mind raced back through fifty years of
always loving you.

We were just kids, "It'll never last" was
what we heard them say,
But last it did and here we are on this
our darkest day.

The Doctor said to call the kids… you'd not
last through the night

We stood and prayed beside your bed,
and wondered at your plight.

Sometimes I cried, sometimes I prayed, I screamed
out in despair.
Why did this happen? Where are you God? Tell me,
Tell me, where?

I felt His touch as he calmed my mind, how could
I not believe?
I'd never have dreamed the help and support
and blessings I would receive.

I was standing there, beside your bed, God, let him
wake up please!
I held your hand and silently prayed, suddenly
I felt a squeeze!

You looked at me with a far off stare, but I knew
I had you back.
Our love had survived another test, this love
would never lack.

Many days have come and gone, since that
last motorcycle ride,
The road's been long; the way's been hard,
our patience really tried.

I do not know what lies ahead in the days and
months to come,
But come what may, we will go on, for together
we have won!

BJH
2006

Sleep

What shall close my eyes in sleep?
Who shall dare my dreams to keep?
When I'm in slumber late at night,
To where do all my thoughts take flight?

With eyes closed in sleepy slumber,
Ears can't hear the deepest thunder.
Minds are void with nothing there,
Souls are free to walk on air.

A new day breaks, so fresh and bright,
Dark gives way to glorious light.
Minds and thoughts and souls conform,
Life is back to the usual norm.

BJH
07/10/01

The Journey

I'll take you to a meadow where buttercups abound.

I'll take you to a babbling brook to bask in the sound.

    I'll take you to a mountain top where all the
        world looks new.

    I'll take you deep within my heart where my
        love grows for you.

If you can see the buttercups as they glow upon my face,

And wade out in the water as you wonder at its pace,

    You'll find yourself above the clouds, the sky
        a purest blue.

    You'll know within your own heart, my love
        is forever true.

BJH
2003
Written for my husband, Jerry

A Mother's Journey

A Mother's journey takes a path where others
fear to tread.
A Mother's job is never done; I've often heard it said.
The very first time a babe is laid on Mother's
breast with care,
A void is filled within her heart just knowing he is there.

The bond between a Mother and child is
hard to understand.
It's never broken even though the boy becomes a man.
No one ever loved a child exactly like its mother,
Search the world for a greater love, there simply
is no other.

A paper cut or a skinned up knee, her kiss will fix it all.
Her ears are tuned to the slightest sound if her
little ones should call.
She never rests until she knows her brood is safe at home.
The need to "Mother" will never stop even when
they're fully grown.

Her love will go from the deepest depths to the highest
mountain peak,
And an easier path for her child to trod is
something she will seek.
To lend a hand or give advice, she learns to
know "just when"
Such diplomacy and tactfulness is never achieved by men.

This journey I've been traveling has taken many years.
Sometimes the road was rough to walk,
sometimes there were tears.

But I've been blessed beyond compare with
three boys and a girl,
They've warmed my heart, they've made me proud,
they've set my life a whirl.

So if the time has not arrived for you to be called Mom,
Be patient dear, do not fret, that time will surly come.
God will grant you little ones, as precious as can be,
And you will walk that sacred path upon you own journey.

BJH
04/22/02

Written for a Mother/Daughter Banquet

Ryan

On September the 18th, the year '84
I became Grandma, who could ask for more?

Through the nursery window I looked at you there,
All wiggly and wrinkled, naked and bare.

The nurses were busy getting you dressed,
I swelled with pride, I must confess.

All those years my name was Mother
And in my heart, there could be no other.

All of a sudden on that glorious day,
"Hey, there's Grandma" I heard them all say!

Are they really talking about me?
Yes, I was Grandma, it was plain to see.

You were so special, my first Grandchild,
I knew I could hold you in just a short while.

Of all my Grandsons, you were first born,
Our hearts had a bond that could not be torn.

Even though you are grown and taller than me,
That bond is still there, so plain to see.

My prayers go with you each step that you take,
In every decision and plan that you make.

**May God keep you in the palm of His hand,
I'm proud of this boy...I'm proud of this man.**

**BJH
2003**

From my Heart and Soul

Brandon

He saw your tiny fingers before they came to be.
He knew that they'd hold drumsticks
even before you turned three.
He gave you a love for music,
A rare talent hard to find.

He made your body big and tall,
a heart compassionate and kind.
Oh, I know that I'm your Nana
who sees through prejudiced eyes,
but the love and kindness you show forth
Is not a mere disguise.

I pray God guides your footsteps
through all your life's long days,
And never fail to thank Him
For His goodness to you always.

I'm proud of all your accomplishments
And the young man you've become.
And I'll not forget to thank Him
For such a fine Grandson.

BJH
2003
In honor of Brandon's graduation

Sam

There once was a couple so happy and free
But something was missing it was plain to see.
They had each other and a love of pure gold
But there was no baby to love and to hold.

For more than 10 years they hoped and they prayed
But the void was still there and stayed and stayed.
God had worked, in a time of His own,
Their prayers had been heard, a seed had been sown.

The couple was called……we found you a baby,
He would be born to a precious lady.
On the cold afternoon of February twelfth,
The baby was born in very good health.

His Mother was single and all alone,
No way to tend to a child of her own.
She signed the papers, he was given a name.
The couple's life…..never the same.

Never blood of our blood even from the start,
But Sam became more he was heart of our heart.
He became Grandson he was number six,
Put them together, they're really a mix.

We love him the same as the five born before,
He has brought this family much happiness and joy.

Memorial Tribute

We have gathered together from far and wide
And locally around the countryside.
To celebrate this special day,
Memorial Reunion in the month of May.

With laughs and hugs and even some tears
We reminisce down through the years.
It's hard to believe how the children have grown,
Yet by their traits they are still known.

As we look at faces from far and near,
It brings a remembrance of those not here.
But they're celebrating in a better place,
Because of God's Amazing Grace.

Their spirits are happy and they feel no pain,
They'll never cry or feel sorrow again.

Until it's time for us to go,
We'll carry on, because we know;

That someday we'll join them around the throne,
And this new place we will all call "Home."

BJH
1995

Written for the Holt/Childers Reunion
Memorial Day Weekend 1999

Happy Mother's Day

I very seldom tell you, just what you mean to me.
For loving me, raising me, to what I've come to be.
I tried to teach my children to be honest, gentle and kind,
I can still hear your teachings in the back of my mind.

Mothers and Daughters have a way of revolving
through the years,
I have heard my daughter repeat the words
That came from my mouth and from yours.
When I was young, people said,
"you're just like your Mother."
What better compliment could they pay?
There simply is no other.

Now they say it to my girl and I hope she feels the same,
I'd rather they know that I'm her Mom, than
be called by my own name.
I hope my love for you, Mother, is very plain to see,
But just to let you know for sure, you're my cup of tea!

BJH
2001

Friends

*Friends come in different shapes and different sizes too.
Friends seem to find, the time to always see us through.*

*Throughout this walk upon the earth,
We meet along the way,
Acquaintances start, friendship begins,
And grows from day to day.*

*I'm glad my path has crossed with yours
As I've walked these many miles,
You've made me laugh, cheered me up
And brought me many smiles.*

*May God bless you is my prayer,
you've been a good friend to me.
May He keep you in His hands,
Until His face we see.*

**BJH
May 2003**

Our Love

We have stood together for 43 years.
This time has brought us happiness and tears.
So swiftly the years have passed away
but our love is stronger even today.

You've brought me joy beyond compare
your love has made me walk on air.
We have memories I will never forget
and I'll always be your loving "Bet".

Love letters, poems and get-away trips
from the cup of love, how we have sipped.
Those sweet nothings you'd say in my ear
within your arms, I had nothing to fear.

We've raised a family of really good kids
they've made us proud of things they did.
Six grandsons have made our life a whirl
but I pray the next one...Please God... Is a girl!

Another 43 years? Certainly I say!
But we will settle for just "day by day."
Our love has stood the test of time
and is finer than sweet, sweet wine.

On the horizon the sun's 'bout to set
seems just a short time since we first met.
Our vision has dimmed, our hair's turning gray
that we leave here together is what I pray.

From my Heart and Soul

*My sweet Jerry, you're the love of my life,
I have been proud to be called your wife.
We are so blessed this Anniversary day
and together forever, may we stay.*

With all my love, "Bet" February 14, 2002

Financial Supporters

I want to thank the following people for placing their trust in me, by giving of their finances and for their prayerful support. Without you, this book would still be in manuscript form. God Bless You All!

Pat Smith	James and Martha Qualls
Deborah Allen	Bishop Charles and Darla Tate
Ruby Smith	Bernie and Melissa Gibbs
Sandy Lange	Mike and Linda Little
Peggy Holt	Russell and Johnna Lee
Jenny Douglas	Jamie and Julie Weaver
Aggie Pavone	Terry and Rebecca Brandon
Cindy Todd Neimeyer	Jim and Linda Meherg
Michelle Dolley	Ken, Debbie and Sam Holt
Marilyn Hughes	Jeff, Sherle and Nicholas Holt
Debbie Bock	Harles and Janet Holt
Lynda Lawson	Bob and Linda Holt
Marilyn Loudermilk	Jack, Lisa and Tyler Summers
Debra Tyler	Ryan and Emily Summers
Steven Holt	Kyle and Megan Summers
Jeremy Holt	Hubert and Pam Burden
Brandon Holt	Sid and Shirley Beaird
Peggy Ramer	Al and Priscilla Ortiz
Nina Fairfield	Vern and Hazel Giltner

Ruth Turner	Jay and Illa Miller
Carlos and Mildred White	Steve and Pat Giltner
Bob and Johnie Paterson	James and Paula Chapman
Ralph and Jane Call	David and Debbie Brannum
David and Ginger Rickman	J. B. and Kay Felts
Steve Childers	Tim Childers

I want to give a special thank you to Megan Summers for doing the picture layouts for me.